Ready-to-Use

SOCIAL SKILLS LESSONS & ACTIVITIES

for Grades 7–12

 **RUTH WELTMANN BEGUN, Editor**
The Society for Prevention of Violence
with
The Center for Applied Research in Education

A ready-to-use curriculum based on real-life situations to help you
build student's self-esteem, self-control, respect for the
rights of others, and a sense of responsibility for one's own actions.

**THE CENTER FOR APPLIED
RESEARCH IN EDUCATION**
West Nyack, New York 10994

Library of Congress Cataloging-in-Publication Data

Ready-to-use social skills lessons & activities for grades 7–12
      Ruth Weltmann Begun, editor ; with The Center for Applied Research in
Education.
          p.   cm. — (Social skills curriculum activities library)
      Includes bibliographical references.
      ISBN 0-87628-866-2
      1. Social skills—Study and teaching (Secondary)—Activity
programs.   2. Social skills—Outlines, syllabi, etc.   3. Social
interaction in adolescence.   I. Begun, Ruth Weltmann.   II. Center for
Applied Research in Education.   III. Series.
      HQ783.R394   1995   95-37635
      646.7′0071′2—dc20   CIP

Printed in the United States of America

10   9   8

ISBN 0-87628-866-2

**THE CENTER FOR APPLIED RESEARCH
IN EDUCATION**
West Nyack, NY 10994

On the World Wide Web at http://www.phdirect.com

ABOUT THIS SOCIAL SKILLS TEACHING RESOURCE

Today's educators carry added responsibilities because significant social changes have had an impact on human relations. Family ties have been loosened. The number of single-parent families has grown. Stresses in many families are often high. Thus, youngsters are frequently exposed to influences that tend to make them aggressive and possibly violent. Moreover, television, now in almost every home, frequently shows events not suitable for guiding children. Youngsters who cannot read and write watch violent scenes and might draw wrong conclusions. Unless schools, daycare centers, head start programs, and parents counteract asocial influences starting at the pre-kindergarten level, verbal and physical interpersonal abuse and violence will be an increasing problem.

This resource is one of four books in the "Social Skills Curriculum Activities Library," a practical series designed to help teachers, care givers, and parents in giving children regular social skills lessons. The full Library spans all grade levels, preschool through grade 12, and includes:

READY-TO-USE SOCIAL SKILLS LESSONS & ACTIVITIES FOR GRADES PreK-K
READY-TO-USE SOCIAL SKILLS LESSONS & ACTIVITIES FOR GRADES 1-3
READY-TO-USE SOCIAL SKILLS LESSONS & ACTIVITIES FOR GRADES 4-6
READY-TO-USE SOCIAL SKILLS LESSONS & ACTIVITIES FOR GRADES 7-12

Each grade-level book provides 50 or more detailed, age-appropriate lessons for developing specific social skills accompanied by reproducible activity sheets and other activities to help students learn the skill. The lessons are presented in a uniform format and follow a Structured Learning approach to teach the skills. They focus on real situations in children's own lives, such as dealing with feelings and peer pressure, and are readily adapted for use in any classroom, school, or home setting.

The lessons and activities in Books 1, 2, and 3 are followed by two special sections entitled "Social Skills Task Review" and "Social Skills Family Training Booklet." "Social Skills Task Review" presents 21 social skills topics that can be used for teacher-led discussions during Circle Time. These are printed in the form of discussion cards that can be photocopied and cut out for use at the appropriate time. You can introduce each topic once before studying a skill and later, following the lesson, to measure what children have learned. The "Social Skills Family Training Booklet" is addressed to parents and single pages can be copied as needed for use with individual children. The booklet includes a brief introduction to its purposes and acknowledgment to its originators followed by a family social skills checklist, and helpful hints and reminders for using the booklet and teaching social skills effectively. The heart of the booklet is comprised of "Fourteen Selected Social Skills" with suggested skill activities that can be done within the family.

NOTE: Copies of the booklet can be ordered from the publisher, The Center for Applied Research in Education, at the minimum quantity of 20.

The lessons and activities in Book 4 are followed by a different format of the "Social Skills Task Review." In Book 4, forty social skills topics are addressed in the form of printed questions. They can be used for discussion and serve the same purpose as the cards. The "Social Skills Family Training Booklet" is not included in Book 4, but copies can be ordered.

Most of the lessons and activities in the Social Skills Library were written, edited, and classroom-tested by teachers from the Cleveland (Ohio) Public Schools in cooperation with faculty from John Carroll University's Department of Education. The project was funded by The Society for Prevention of Violence (SPV), a non-profit organization founded by S. J. Begun, Ph.D., and his wife Ruth Weltmann Begun, M.S., and sponsored by them and various contributing corporations and foundations. Specific credits are given on the Acknowledgments page.

Major objectives of teaching these lessons are to build students' self-esteem, self-control, respect for the rights of others, and a sense of responsibility for one's own actions. Another objective is to teach the students to settle grievances and conflicts through communication without recourse to violence. We believe that such training can be effective and successful by increasing discipline and reducing the drop-out rate. Thus, students will benefit from social skills training throughout their lives.

S. J. Begun, Ph.D.

Ruth Weltmann Begun, M.S.

The Society for Prevention of Violence

Self-image improved

Only giving compliments

Completing tasks

Ignoring distractions

Anger dealt with

Less aggression

Seatwork and homework done

Keep following classroom rules

Ignoring teasing

Leave a troublesome situation

Learning to accept consequences

Staying out of fights

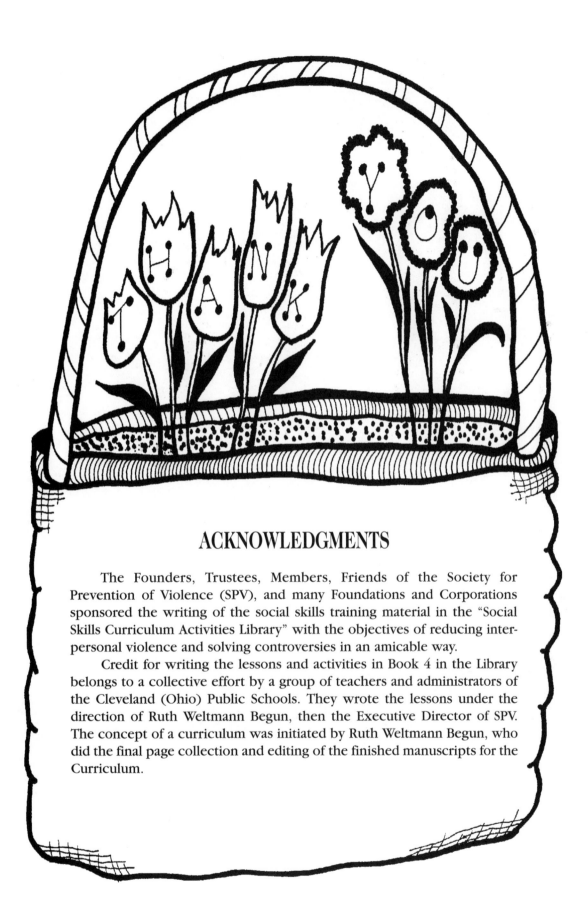

ACKNOWLEDGMENTS

The Founders, Trustees, Members, Friends of the Society for Prevention of Violence (SPV), and many Foundations and Corporations sponsored the writing of the social skills training material in the "Social Skills Curriculum Activities Library" with the objectives of reducing interpersonal violence and solving controversies in an amicable way.

Credit for writing the lessons and activities in Book 4 in the Library belongs to a collective effort by a group of teachers and administrators of the Cleveland (Ohio) Public Schools. They wrote the lessons under the direction of Ruth Weltmann Begun, then the Executive Director of SPV. The concept of a curriculum was initiated by Ruth Weltmann Begun, who did the final page collection and editing of the finished manuscripts for the Curriculum.

ABOUT THE SOCIETY FOR PREVENTION OF VIOLENCE (SPV)

The Society for Prevention of Violence (SPV) is dedicated to reducing the prevalence of violent acts and asocial behaviors in children and adults through education. It accomplishes this mission by teaching children and adults the use of skills necessary to build their character, helping them acquire a strong values system, motivating them to develop their communication skills and to realize growth in interpersonal relationships. The mission includes integration of social and academic skills to encourage those who use them to reach their full potential and contribute to our nation's society by being able to make decisions and solve problems through effective and appropriate means.

As a non-profit organization, the Society had its origin in 1972 as the Begun Institute for the Study of Violence and Aggression at John Carroll University (Cleveland, Ohio). A multitude of information was gathered, studied, and analyzed during the ensuing ten-year period. Symposia were held which involved numerous well-known presenters and participants from various career fields. Early on, the founders of the Institute, S. J. and Ruth Begun, foresaw the trend of increasing violence in our families, communities, and across the nation, and chose to take a leadership role in pioneering an educational approach to help alleviate aggressive and antisocial behavior. The educational approach was and continues to be the sole *PROACTIVE* means to change behaviors. Current conditions reflect our society's reliance on reactive means of dealing with this problem. During the next ten-year period, through the determination and hard work of Ruth Weltmann Begun as executive director, the workshops, parent training sessions, collaborative projects, and a comprehensive (preschool through grade 12) Social Skills Training Curriculum were developed.

Today, classroom teachers in numerous school districts across the country are utilizing this internationally recognized curriculum. The Society continually seeks support through individual donors, grants, direct paid services, and material/consultant service sales. It also has expanded its involvement in the educational process by:

- publishing a semiannual newsletter and other pertinent articles;
- providing inservice training for professional staffs, parents, and others;
- providing assistance in resource identification, proposal writing/project design, and evaluation;
- tailoring instructional (academic and other) delivery designs to specific school/organization needs; and
- implementing pilot demonstration projects with foundation support.

As we move into and through the twenty-first century, we must work diligently and cooperatively to turn challenges into successes.

The Society also offers graduate-level workshops in cooperation with John Carroll University for educators. Credits earned in these workshops may be applied toward renewal of certificates through the Ohio Department of Education.

For further information, contact The Society for Prevention of Violence, 3439 West Brainard Road #102, Woodmere, Ohio 44122 (phone 216/591-1876) or 3109 Mayfield Road, Cleveland Heights, Ohio 44118 (phone 216/371-5545).

ABOUT THE SOCIAL SKILLS CURRICULUM

Philosophy

We believe that the learning of social skills is the foundation for social and academic adequacy. It assists in the prevention of social problems and leads to successful functioning and survival skills for our citizens. Social behavior and academic behavior are highly correlated. We believe it is more productive to teach children the proper ways to behave than to admonish them for improper behavior. This requires direct and systematic teaching, taking into consideration social and developmental theory in the affective, cognitive, and psycho-motor domains. Learning should be sequential, linked to community goals, and consistent with behaviors that are relevant to student needs. This social skills curriculum is based on these beliefs.

Curriculum Overview

As children grow, one way they learn social behaviors is by watching and interacting with other people. Some children who have failed to learn appropriate behaviors have lacked opportunities to imitate good role models, have received insufficient or inappropriate reinforcement, or have misunderstood adequate social experiences.

The Social Skills Curriculum is designed to teach these behaviors in ways that correlate with child development theory, namely how children learn in their natural environment. Each lesson provides models for children to imitate and correction strategies following practice of the skills. The teacher and the rest of the class then provide positive reinforcement to encourage the continued use of the appropriate skills in situations that occur in any environment.

Teachers using this curriculum can be flexible. The curriculum is designed to be used in the classroom as lessons taught for about 20-30 minutes, two to three times a week. However, it is not the intent that these be the only times social skills are taught and learned. Every opportunity should be used to reinforce, model, and coach the children so that they can practice the skills enough to feel comfortable with them as part of their ways of behaving. Therefore, the teacher should remind the students of the skills and the need to use them in all appropriate situations once the skills have been demonstrated. The teacher should also plan to model the skills in any and all interactions with the children. The teacher should be *consistent* in not only using the skills when they are taught, but in using them in all interactions with the students. Only this kind of consistent modeling will assure that the children will see the skills used repeatedly and begin to know and feel comfortable with using them. Teachers should also feel free to adapt the material to class needs and to design and develop strategies, models, and interventions other than those suggested here. Students can even be involved in helping to think of modeling strategies and other techniques.

The Social Skills Curriculum Library is graded pre-Kindergarten through Grade Twelve and presented in four books focusing on four different levels: grades preK-K, 1-3, 4-6, and 7-12. It uses a structured learning approach to teach the skills. *Structured Learning* is a holistic teaching method that provides a framework for systematic teaching in a way that is similar to the academic model. The emphasis in this curriculum is to provide constructive and structured behaviors for socially skill-deficient children.

Structured Learning consists of *four basic components*: modeling, role playing, discussion of performance, and use in real-life situations. For more effective teaching, the lessons include eight steps that follow a directed lesson format (see below):

Social Skill: A social behavior that is directly observable.

Behavioral Objective: An expected outcome of learning the social skill that can be evaluated.

Directed Lesson: Each behavior is defined and stated in observable terms; the behavior is demonstrated and practiced; a student's level of performance is evaluated and inappropriate behaviors are corrected. Positive reinforcement is used to encourage continued use of the skill in all areas of the student's environment.

1. ***Establish the Need:*** The purpose of teaching the lesson is included. What benefits will learning the skill provide? What are the consequences of not learning the behavior?

2. ***Introduction:*** Stories, poems, puppets, and questions are used to make the social skill more concrete to the children.

3. ***Identify the Skill Components:*** These skill steps are used to teach the behavior. By following and practicing these steps, the student will be able to demonstrate the behavior when needed.

4. ***Model the Skill:*** The teacher or socially adept child demonstrates the appropriate behaviors so that the students can imitate them. The skill components are referred to during the modeling.

5. ***Behavioral Rehearsal:*** The children are given an opportunity to perform the behavior which can be evaluated, corrected, and reinforced.

    A. ***Selection***—The teacher selects participants or asks for volunteers. The number of children depends on the time allowed and whatever is appropriate for each lesson.

    B. ***Role Play***—The participants are assigned their roles or situations they will role play.

    C. ***Completion***—This is a means to determine that the role playing is complete. After each role play, reinforce correct behaviors, identify inappropriate behaviors, and reenact role play with corrections. If there are no corrections, role play is complete.

    D. ***Reinforcers***—Positive reinforcement by the teacher and the class is used for maintenance of the skill. Various methods can be used: verbal encouragement, tangible rewards, special privileges, and keeping a record of social and academic improvement.

    E. ***Discussion***—The student's level of performance is evaluated and inappropriate behaviors are corrected. How did the participants feel while performing? What difficulties might be faced in implementing the skill? What observations did the class make?

6. ***Practice:*** Activities that help the children summarize the skill. The practice can be done by using worksheets, doing art projects, making film strips, writing stories, keeping diaries and charts, and so on.

7. ***Independent Use:*** Activities that help facilitate the use of these behaviors outside the school environment. Family and friends take an active role in reinforcing the importance of using these alternative behaviors in a conflict situation.

8. ***Continuation:*** At the end of each lesson, the teacher reminds the class that applying social skills can benefit them in academic and social relationships. Stress that although there are difficulties in applying the skills (such as in regard to negative peer pressure), the benefits outweigh the problems. One such benefit is more self-confidence in decision-making. Maintaining social behavior is an ongoing process. It requires teachers to show appropriate behaviors and reinforce them when they are demonstrated.

STRUCTURED LEARNING

FOUR BASIC COMPONENTS

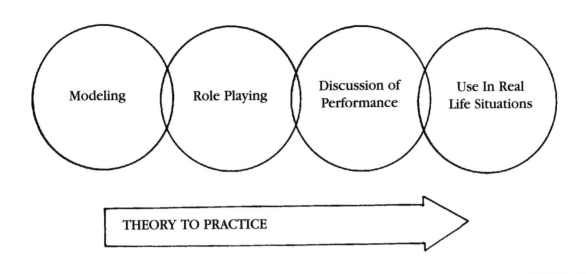

Modeling   Role Playing   Discussion of Performance   Use In Real Life Situations

THEORY TO PRACTICE

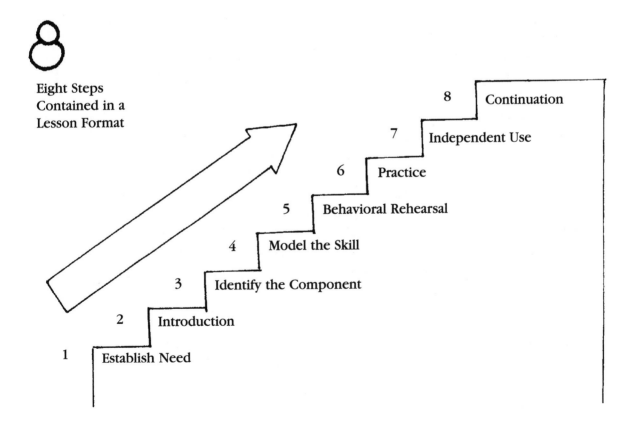

Eight Steps
Contained in a
Lesson Format

8 Continuation

7 Independent Use

6 Practice

5 Behavioral Rehearsal

4 Model the Skill

3 Identify the Component

2 Introduction

1 Establish Need

BIBLIOGRAPHY

Books

Apter, Stephen J., and Arnold P. Goldstein. *Youth Violence: Program and Prospects.* Needham Heights, MA: Allyn & Bacon, 1986.

Ballare, Antonia, and Angelique Lampros. *Behavior Smart! Ready-to-Use Activities for Building Personal and Social Skills for Grades K-4.* West Nyack, NY: Center for Applied Research in Education, 1994.

Cartledge, Gwendolyn, and Joanne Fellows Milburn. *Teaching Social Skills to Children,* 2nd ed. Needham Heights, MA: Allyn & Bacon, 1986.

Cherry, Clare. *Please Don't Sit on the Kids: Alternatives to Punitive Discipline.* Belmont, CA: Fearon-Pitman, 1982.

Chirinian, Helene. *Cartoon Comprehension.* Redondo Beach, CA: Frank Schaeffer Publications, 1980.

Eberle, Bob. *Help! in Managing Your Classroom.* Carthage, IL: Good Apple, 1984.

Farnette, C., I. Forte, and B. Loss. *I've Got Me and I'm Glad.* rev. ed. Nashville, TN: Incentive Publications, 1989.

Feshbach, Norma, and Seymour Feshbach et al. *Learning to Care: Classroom Activities for Social and Affective Development.* Glenview, IL: Good Year Books, 1983.

Gerne, Timothy A. and Patricia J. *Substance Abuse Prevention Activities for Elementary Children.* Englewood Cliffs, NJ: Prentice Hall, 1986. *Substance Abuse Activities for Secondary Students.* Englewood Cliffs, NJ: Prentice Hall, 1991.

Ginott, Haim G. *Teacher and Child, A Book for Parents.* New York: Macmillan, 1984.

Goldstein, Arnold P., Stephen J. Apter, and Berj Harootunian. *School Violence.* Englewood Cliffs, NJ: Prentice Hall, 1984.

Goldstein, Arnold P. et al. *Skillstreaming the Adolescent: A Structured Learning Approach to Teaching Prosocial Skills.* Champaign, IL: Research Press, 1980.

Grevious, Saundrah Clark. *Ready-to-Use Multicultural Activities for Primary Children.* West Nyack, NY: Center for Applied Research in Education, 1993.

Kaplan, P.G., S.K. Crawford, and S.L. Nelson. *Nice.* Denver: Love, 1977.

Mannix, Darlene. *Be a Better Student: Lessons and Worksheets for Teaching Behavior Management in Grades 4-9.* West Nyack, NY: Center for Applied Research in Education, 1989.

—. *Life Skills Activities for Special Children.* West Nyack, NY: Center for Applied Research in Education, 1991.

—. *Social Skills Activities for Special Children.* West Nyack, NY: Center for Applied Research in Education, 1993.

McElmurry, Mary Ann. *Caring.* Carthage, IL: Good Apple, 1981.

—. *Feelings.* Carthage, IL: Good Apple, 1981.

McGinnis, Ellen, and Arnold P. Goldstein. *Skillstreaming the Elementary School Child: A Guide for Teaching Prosocial Skills.* Champaign, IL: Research Press, 1984.

Schwartz, Linda. *The Month-to-Month Me.* Santa Barbara, CA: The Learning Works, 1976.

Standish, Bob. *Connecting Rainbows.* Carthage, IL: Good Apple, 1982.

Stephens, Thomas M. *Social Skills in the Classroom,* 2nd ed. Lutz, FL: Psychological Assessment Resources, 1992.

Stull, Elizabeth Crosby. *Multicultural Discovery Activities for the Elementary Grades.* West Nyack, NY: Center for Applied Research in Education, 1994.

Teolis, Beth. *Ready-to-Use Self-Esteem Activities for Grades 4-8.* West Nyack, NY: Center for Applied Research in Education, 1995.

Toner, Patricia Rizzo. *Relationships and Communication Activities.* West Nyack, NY: Center for Applied Research in Education, 1993.

—. *Stress Management and Self-Esteem Activities.* West Nyack, NY: Center for Applied Research in Education, 1993.

Documents

Early Identification of Classification of Juvenile Delinquents: Hearing Before the Subcommittee on the Constitution. U.S. Senate, 97th Congress; Serial No. J-97-70; October 22, 1981; Testimony by: Gerald R. Patterson, Research Scientist—Oregon Social Learning Center, Eugene, Oregon; David Farrington, and John Monahan.

Ounces of Prevention: Toward an Understanding of the Causes of Violence; by State of California Commission on Crime Control and Violence Prevention, 1982.

Sources for Job Skills Lessons

(1) The Application
Your Foot in the Door
Helps reader to make a positive first impression in an interview.
Identified as EM0030, copyright 1991
Order from: Life Skills Education
               Dept. 30
               226 Libbey Parkway
               Weymouth, MA 02189

(2) *Tips for a Successful Interview,* by Dr. Phillip E. Norris and Chip Cooper
Format: Video (22 minutes VHS color)
Order from: JIST WORKS, Inc.
               720 North Park Avenue
               Indianapolis, IN 46202-3431

(3) Job Interview Skills
The Art to Successful Interviewing
Order from: Channing L. Bete Co., Inc.
               200 State Road
               South Deerfield, MA 01373-0200

(4) *Merchandising Your Job Talents,* U.S. Dept. of Labor (1983 rev.),
U.S. Department and Training Administration
Order from: Superintendent of Documents
               U.S. Government Printing Office
               Washington, D.C. 20204

(5) *Career Education,* from the World Book Encyclopedia, copyright 1991,
World Book, Inc.

TABLE OF CONTENTS

SOCIAL SKILLS LESSONS & ACTIVITIES FOR GRADES 7-12

Contents

Contents

SOCIAL SKILLS LESSONS & ACTIVITIES FOR GRADES 7–12

TO THE TEACHER

This section presents 51 ready-to-use social skills lessons with a variety of related activities and worksheets. All of the lessons have been tested and are suggested for use with secondary (grades 7-12) students.

The lessons may be used in any order you desire, though they are sequenced in a general way, beginning with listening skills strategies for the classroom and everyday life. Ultimately, of course, you will match the needs and ability levels of your students with the particular lessons and social skills learning objectives. Some of the lessons may have to be repeated several times over the course of the school year.

You may want to introduce a social skill in a class discussion before presenting the related lesson, as suggested in the "Social Skills Task Review" on pages 204–210. This should give you an idea of how familiar students may or may not be with the skill. The skill can then be discussed by the class following the lesson to see how many students have learned the skill.

The activity sheets accompanying these lessons may be photocopied as many times as you need them for use with individual students, small groups, or the whole class. You may also devise activity sheets of your own to enrich and reinforce any of the lessons.

SOCIAL SKILL
Being a Good Listener

Behavioral Objective: The student will exhibit good listening and concentration skills that are appropriate for classroom learning and everyday life.

Directed Lesson:

1. **Establish the Need:** Stress that listening is one of the most important skills we must learn as young adults. Listening is always necessary in order to understand the needs and desires of others in friendship, adult relationship, and business. We must be able to listen attentively in order to make a living and to understand the problem to be solved.

2. **Introduction:** Read the following story to the students:

   "Sam Jones is on his first day at his first job at Big Jake's. His new boss, Mr. Axle, is having a busy day and would like to help Sam but a busload of campers has just come in for lunch. Sam's first job is to make Big Jake burgers.

   "These are the instructions that Mr. Axle gave him: 'Now Sam, as the burgers come down the line, place the beef patty on the bun first, then add some special sauce, put some onions on it with a slice of tomato, then place the middle bun on, add a slice of cheese, another beef patty, more special sauce, two pickles, and finally a slice of onion.

   "'Oh, and don't forget the lettuce, mustard, ketchup, and relish too! Do you have any questions? Good luck!'

   "Sam was proud to be given so much responsibility the first day. He really wanted to do a good job. Sam started to make his first Big Jake burger. He loved onions and relish, but he didn't like ketchup and mustard. Sam thought the special sauce was tasty on the lettuce.

   "What do you suppose happened to Sam that day? Why?

   "What could he have done in order to have a successful first day?"

3. **Identify the Skill Components:** The teacher lists the following skill components on the board or on sentence strips:

   1. Look at the person who is speaking.
   2. Use positive facial expressions and body language to show that you understand.
   3. Concentrate on what is being said.

1

4. If you are asked a question, indicate that you have heard it by answering or nodding your head.

5. Ask questions if you do not understand or need additional information.

4. **Model the Skill:** Teacher models the skill by having a student reenact the situation at Big Jake's. Show the students how to follow the skill steps. Stress the importance of listening carefully to everything said.

5. **Behavioral Rehearsal:**

   A. *Selection:* Ask students to form several small groups of three to role play.

   B. *Role Play:* Ask each group to role play the situation at Big Jake's. Have the class critique each group to see how well each set of students fared in listening to directions.

   C. *Completion:* After each role play, reinforce correct behavior, identify appropriate behaviors, and reenact role play with corrections. If there are no corrections, role play is complete.

   D. *Reinforcers:* Reinforce correct behavior with verbal praise and group reinforcement.

   E. *Discussion:* Discuss how well the role plays were accomplished. Reinforce the skill components.

6. **Practice:** Distribute copies of the following worksheet, "Build a Big Jake," and have students write in the recipe in class.

7. **Independent Use:** Give students copies of the worksheet entitled "Follow a Recipe" and tell them to ask a family member for his or her favorite recipe. The recipe can be from memory or from a cookbook. Try to prepare the dish following their verbal instructions. Complete this project within one week and share the recipe with the class.

8. **Continuation:** As related situations arise, the teacher will point out the importance of listening skills in learning and daily living.

Name _____ Date _____

BUILD A BIG JAKE

DIRECTIONS: On this worksheet write the recipe for your own "BIG JAKE" burger. Then, try to make it at home. Repeat your recipe to a family member and see if they can make your "BIG JAKE" burger.

Name _____ Date _____

FOLLOW A RECIPE

Directions: At home, ask a family member for a recipe that you can make. This recipe can be from a cookbook or from their memory. **Get the necessary ingredients.** Then, have them give the step-by-step process as you prepare the recipe. Good Luck!

SHARE. Write the recipe on the chef's hat below and share it with the class.

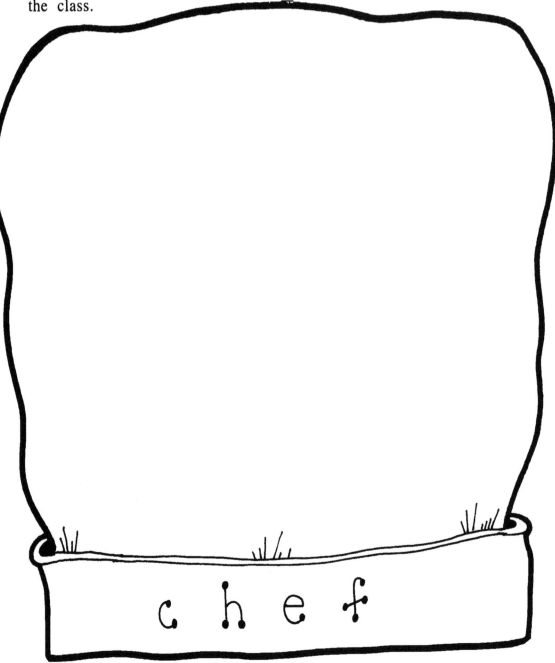

SOCIAL SKILL

Listening to Directions

Behavioral Objective: The student will learn to listen attentively when a person is giving directions.

Directed Lesson:

1. **Establish the Need:** Listening is a skill that is basic to learning. It is a skill that should be learned early as it is needed to participate in class discussions and for following verbal directions.

2. **Introduction:** Tell students to listen carefully to the following story.

> "Carol was excited about her first baby-sitting job. This was an opportunity for her to earn her own money and demonstrate to her parents that she was a responsible person. Carol felt very confident about her abilities for baby-sitting. She had lots of experience caring for her own younger brothers and sisters at home. She felt that she could handle any situation.

> "Carol arrived fifteen minutes early to begin her first job at the home of the Rodgers family. Mrs. Rodgers was pleased with Carol's attitude, appearance, and self-confidence. Mrs. Rodgers explained to Carol that one of her three children suffered violent reactions whenever he ate any food item that had sugar as an ingredient. Mrs. Rodgers asked Carol to listen very carefully to her instructions on how to resolve this problem if it occurred. First, she told her to attempt to calm him down, then give him two teaspoons of medicine and observe him for five minutes to see if it had a calming effect. She added, 'If the condition remains unchanged, give him two more teaspoons of medicine and call me at this phone number.'

> "Carol had never been a good listener, and today was no exception. As Mrs. Rodgers gave these important directions, Carol was playing with the children and patting the family dog on the head.

> "Mr. and Mrs. Rodgers finally departed and Carol was on her own. The first several hours passed without incident. Then, somehow, Johnny, who is allergic to sugar, managed to find a candy bar and ate it. A short time later, Carol heard a crash and other loud noises. Johnny was destructive with his toys and was totally out of control. Carol tried to remember the directions that she had been given by Mrs. Rodgers. She could not remember the sequence of the directions.

> 1. What should Carol do?

> 2. Why is it so important to listen carefully to instructions?"

3. ***Identify the Skill Components:*** List the following skill components on the board or on sentence strips.

    1. Look at the person speaking.

    2. Always concentrate on what is being said.

    3. Respond by nodding or answering questions.

    4. Ask questions if you do not understand or need additional information.

4. ***Model the Skill:*** The teacher, with the assistance of several students, will role play the story. Stress the importance of listening carefully to everything said.

5. ***Behavioral Rehearsal:***

    A. *Selection:* Teacher selects five students to role play.

    B. *Role Play:* Have one student give whispered directions to another student about how to travel from his/her school to a designated point. Continue this process until all students have heard the directions. Then compare the original directions from the first student with the directions given by the last student.

    C. *Completion:* After the role play, reinforce correct behavior, identify inappropriate behaviors, and reenact if needed. Otherwise, the role play is complete.

    D. *Reinforcer:* Teacher and peers should acknowledge appropriate behavior with verbal praise.

    E. *Discussion:* Discuss the effectiveness of the role plays in regard to the students giving the directions and the responses. What could the students who did not listen carefully enough do to correct their behavior?

6. ***Practice:*** Distribute copies of the following worksheet, "Listening," and warn the class to listen carefully. Re-read the story and have the class write down the instructions for baby-sitting with Johnny.

7. ***Independent Use:*** Distribute copies of the worksheet "Baby-Sitting Tips" to the students. Ask them to have an adult family member give them instructions on how to baby-sit. Tell them to see if they can recall the instructions the first time they are given and write them out on their worksheet. They should be prepared to share their answers with the class.

8. ***Continuation:*** The teacher should continue to point out the need for this skill as related situations arise.

Name _____ Date _____

Listening   Listening

LISTENING

Listening   Listening

Directions: How well did you listen to the story? Write down the instructions from the story about baby sitting. Be exact.

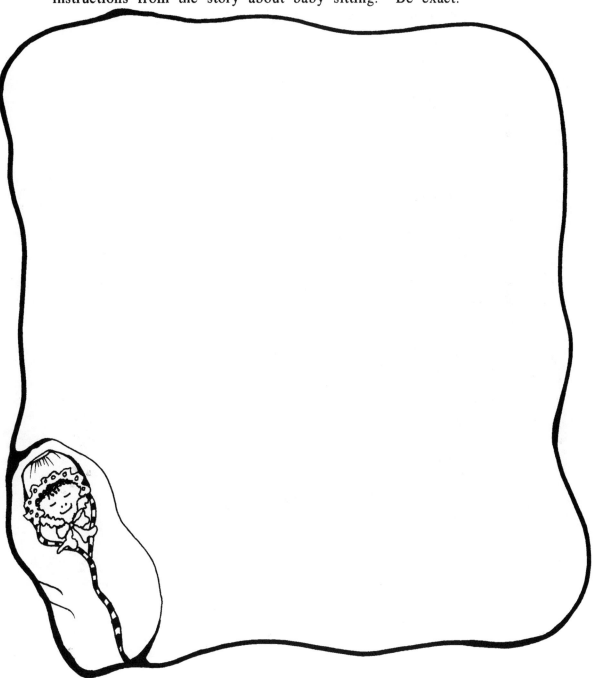

Name _____ Date _____

BABY-SITTING TIPS

Directions: Have an adult family member give you 5 very important instructions to use when you baby-sit. Can you recall the instructions from memory? Write the 5 baby-sitting tips below:

1.

2.

3.

4.

5.

SOCIAL SKILL
Starting a Conversation

Behavioral Objective: The student will recognize the importance of being able to start a conversation properly with a known or unknown person. The student will be able to demonstrate through role playing the difference between proper and improper methods.

Directed Lesson:

1. **Establish the Need:** Starting a conversation is a skill that is basic to being able to communicate with another person. In order to gather information from others, we must be able to start a conversation correctly. Being able to converse is important for landing one's first employment and for keeping the job.

2. **Introduction:** The teacher will ask the class to listen while some different examples of starting a conversation are read.

   "Excuse me, sir, do you have a minute? You look as if you might be able to help me find Park Avenue. Could you give me directions, please?"

   "Hello, Sue. You look very nice in your new dress. Would you like to go out to see a movie?"

   "Excuse me, sir. My name is Bill Smith. I have purchased many of my clothes in your store. It's always pleasant here, and I really like the clothing you have in your store. I would be very interested in working here if you could use some extra help."

3. **Identify the Skill Components:** List the following skill components on the board or print them on sentence strips.

   1. Greet the other individual(s). Face the person(s), and establish eye contact.
   2. Make small talk. Look for things that interest the other person (e.g., in a butcher's shop, you might ask the butcher what his favorite meat is).
   3. Determine if the other person is listening. (Is the other person looking at you, nodding, paying attention?)
   4. Initiate a discussion by starting with topics such as directions, the weather, getting a job, or interest in the other person.
   5. Say, "Hi," shake hands, and compliment the other person's appearance.

4. **Model the Skill:** The teacher will select two students to role-play a situation on starting a conversation. One student must be male and the other female. The situation will involve a male trying to start a conversation with a female.

5. *Behavioral Rehearsal:*

   A. *Selection:* The teacher will select two students for each role play.

   B. *Role Play:* Students will use the following role play:

Joe is a popular male student. He wants to ask Judy out on a date. Judy is shy and wants to go out with Joe, but thinks he is too aggressive. Joe and Judy have just run into each other in the hall after school. Joe says, . . . (start a conversation)."

   C. *Completion:* After each role play, reinforce correct behavior, identify inappropriate behaviors, and reenact role play with corrections. If there are no corrections, role play is complete.

   D. *Reinforcer:* Give verbal praise and group reinforcement.

   E. *Discussion:* Discuss how well the role play was done. Reinforce the skill components.

6. *Practice:* Hand out copies of the following worksheet, "How Would You Start?" and have students complete it in class.

7. *Independent Use:* The student will ask a family member to tell how he/she would start a conversation with the President of the United States. The response will be recorded in writing on the worksheet entitled "A Meeting with the President of the U.S.A." and returned to the teacher within a week.

8. *Continuation:* The teacher will point out the importance of practicing this skill on appropriate occasions as they arise throughout the year.

Name _____ Date _____

HOW WOULD YOU START?

Directions: In the spaces provided below, write down how you would start a conversation with the following people:

 **A. Football Player**

 B. Police Officer

 **C. Doctor**

 **D. A Person at the Bus Stop**

Name _____ Date _____

A MEETING WITH THE PRESIDENT
OF THE U.S.A.

Directions: You have the honor of representing your school at the White House. What is the proper procedure for you to follow? How do you address the President? Look for information. Talk it over with your family and friends.

In the **first** space below, write specific questions. In the **second** space, record answers that you found to be helpful.

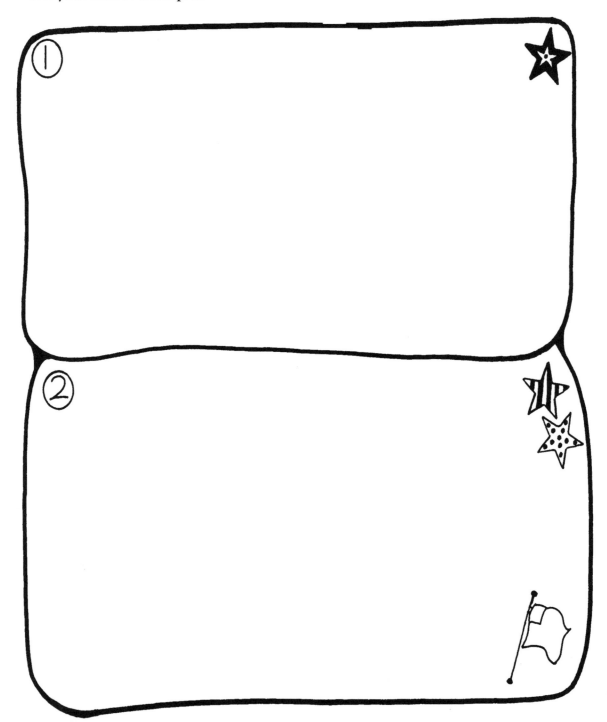

SOCIAL SKILL
Starting a Conversation

Behavioral Objective: The student will recognize the importance of being able to start a conversation properly and demonstrate through role playing the difference between proper and improper use of the skill.

Directed Lesson:

1. **Establish the Need:** Communicating with others is essential for being able to develop relationships and for being successful in the workplace. One must be able to start a conversation in order to find employment.

2. **Introduction:** The teacher will ask the class to listen while some different examples of starting a conversation are read.

   "Excuse me, sir, could you help me? I seem to be lost. Can you direct me to John Carroll University? I have to be there by 6:00 P.M."

   "Hello, Tara. You look very nice today in your bright yellow outfit. I hope you don't mind my asking, but are you busy Saturday night? Maybe we could go see a movie or get a pizza."

   "Excuse me, sir. My name is Luke Walker. Do you have any employment opportunities available? I have a lot of previous experience at a store like this one. Would you possibly consider my application for employment?"

3. **Identify the Skill Components:** List the following skill components on the board or print them on sentence strips.

   1. Greet the other person(s) in a positive manner.
   2. Establish eye contact with the individual(s).
   3. Look for things that are of interest to the other person.
   4. Determine if the other person is listening to you.
   5. Emphasize your main topic of conversation.
   6. Make it clear that you have a point to get across.
   7. Keep the conversation interesting.
   8. Allow the other person to express him/herself.
   9. Listen attentively to the other's point of view.

4. ***Model the Skill:*** The teacher will select two students to role play a situation where one student is starting a conversation. One student can be male and the other female.

5. ***Behavioral Rehearsal:***

   A. *Selection:* The teacher will select two students for each role play.

   B. *Role Play:* Students will use the following role play situations:

   - asking for directions to a particular location
   - looking for a lost pet dog
   - starting a conversation at a bus stop
   - starting a conversation on the bus with the person sitting next to you

   C. *Completion:* After each role play, reinforce the correct behavior. Identify inappropriate behavior and reenact role play with corrections. If there are no corrections, role play is complete.

   D. *Reinforcers:* Reinforce correct behavior with verbal praise and group reinforcement.

   E. *Discussion:* Discuss how well the role play was done. Reinforce the skill components.

6. ***Practice:*** Distribute copies of the following worksheet, "What Would *You* Say?", and have students complete it in class.

7. ***Independent Use:*** Give students copies of the worksheet "Talking with the Mayor" and have them ask a family member to tell how they would start a conversation with the mayor of a large city. Students should record the answer and return the worksheet on an assigned date.

8. ***Continuation:*** During the year, the teacher can recall and highlight this skill whenever the situation calls for it.

Name _____ Date _____

WHAT WOULD *YOU* SAY?

Directions: In the spaces provided, write down some possible "conversation starters" if you should meet the following people:

Baseball Player

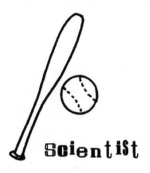

Scientist

Lawyer

Neighbor

Name _____ Date _____

TALKING WITH THE MAYOR

Directions: You have an opportunity to meet the Mayor of your city. Here is an opportunity to discuss issues facing your school. In the space below, write specific points that you would like to make.

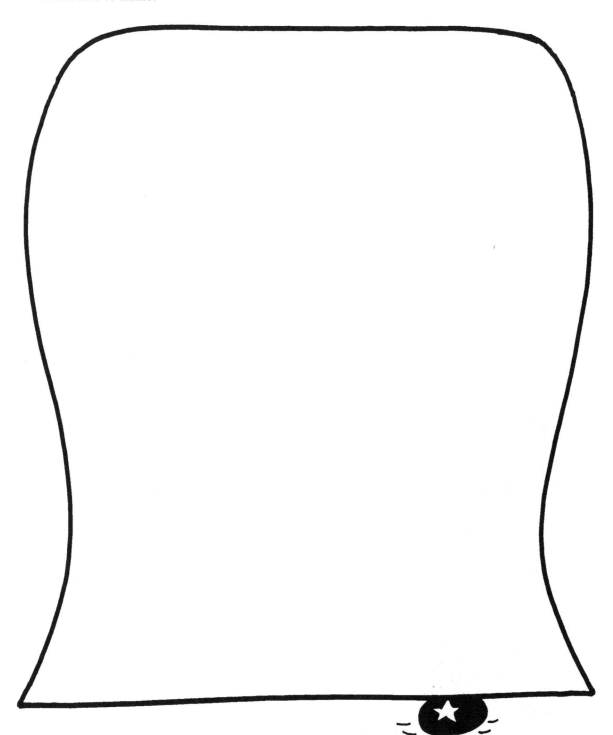

SOCIAL SKILL
Asking for Help in Class

Behavioral Objective: The student will learn to ask for help when needed.

Directed Lesson:

1. **Establish the Need:** Asking for help is an essential part of the learning experience. This is a skill every student needs in order to be successful in school as well as at home, with peers, or at work.

2. **Introduction:** Read this story to the class:

   "Mr. Jones had just introduced his math class to positive and negative integers. He then gave the class a homework assignment on the subject of integers. One of the students, John, didn't really understand integers at all. He wrote down the assignment, but when Mr. Jones asked if there were any questions, John was silent. The next day John didn't turn in his assignment."

   The teacher asks the class: **"Why do you think John was unable to complete his assignment?"**

3. **Identify the Skill Components:** Write the following on the board or on sentence strips.

   1. Decide what the problem is.
   2. Decide if you want help to solve the problem.
   3. Find the right person to help you.
   4. Ask that person for help.
   5. Use the suggestion to solve your problem.

4. **Model the Skill:** The teacher will ask volunteers from the class to share some experiences about situations when they needed help, and to list these situations on the board. The class will then have a discussion about asking for help by using the five basic skill components.

5. **Behavioral Rehearsal:**

   A. *Selection:* Teacher selects three groups of three students each to role play.

   B. *Role Play:* The groups will role play the different situations suggested by the class. The rest of the class will watch for the steps as listed in the skill components.

   C. *Completion:* After each role play, reinforce correct behaviors, identify inappropriate behaviors, and reenact role play with corrections. If there are no corrections, role play is complete.

    D. *Reinforcers:* Verbal praise from teachers and peers and improved social and academic skills provide effective reinforcement.

    E. *Discussion:* Critique not only how the role players focused on the skills but how well the audience critiqued the role playing situations.

6. ***Practice:*** Distribute copies of the following worksheet, "Asking for Help," and ask students to write down four situations they have encountered recently when they needed help to find a solution. They will then choose one of those situations as a way of modeling the skill, list the five steps in modeling the skill, and follow up with appropriate actions for each step.

7. ***Independent Use:*** Students will practice asking for help in real life situations using the guidelines in the worksheet entitled "Real Life Drama." They will report back to the class verbally and in writing on the steps they used and the result of their efforts.

8. ***Continuation:*** Teacher will point out that people who learn to ask for help when needed will not feel inadequate, but will feel more confident and become better skilled in all areas.

Name _____ Date _____

ASKING FOR HELP

I. List 4 situations when you needed help in completing a task or understanding a concept. (These situations do *not* have to be school-related.)

    1._____

    2._____

    3._____

    4._____

II. Copy the 5 skill components from the board.

    1._____

    2._____

    3._____

    4._____

    5._____

III. Choose one of the situations you listed at the top of the page. Use the skill components and decide how you would get help for solving this problem.

Complete the "Asking for Help" cartoon strip on the next page.

Name _____ Date _____

ASKING FOR HELP - cartoon

Directions: Complete each step of the cartoon using one of the four situations in which you needed and wanted help.

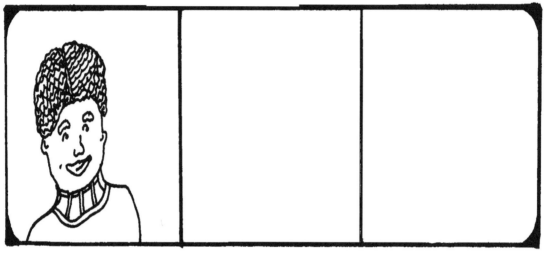

1. Name the Problem   **2. Do I Want Help?**   **3. Who Will Help Me?**

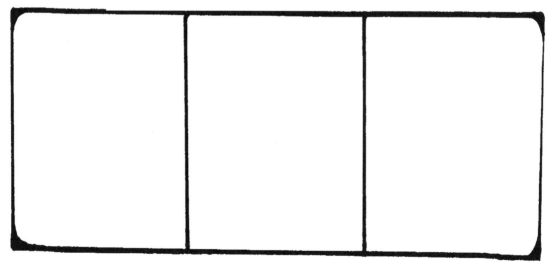

4. Ask Someone   **5. Use the Suggestions**   **6. A Happier Me**

Name _____ Date _____

REAL LIFE DRAMA

1. I really needed help when:

_____

_____

_____

_____

2. I chose _____ to help me with this problem.

3. _____ suggested that I

_____

_____

_____

_____

4. I followed the suggestions.

First, I _____

_____

_____

_____

SOCIAL SKILL
Asking for Help When Needed

Behavioral Objective: The student will learn to ask for help when needed, especially when dealing with sexual feelings, the loss of a loved one, or peer pressure.

Directed Lesson:

1. **Establish the Need:** As young people mature, those who learn to ask for help when needed are the ones who are most likely to succeed. This age group is especially reluctant to seek help when needed. Faced with problems such as early sexual involvement, drug usage, and suicide attempts, they need to know that help is available.

2. **Introduction:** Read the following story to the class:

   "Martha and Patricia live on the east side of town. They made friends with Helen and Janice who live on the west side. One weekend, they all made plans to get together and go shopping. Martha and Patricia decided to meet their friends at the mall on the west side.

   "They weren't sure of bus routes and schedules, so they left early. When it was time to change buses, Martha was sure they should take the express bus, but Patricia thought the local bus would be better. It was time to get on the bus and there were three buses waiting there. The girls just decided to get on the first bus in line.

   "Well, it turned out that their bus didn't go anywhere near the mall. The girls spent half the day riding that bus waiting for it to return to where they first got on. Of course, Janice and Helen got tired of waiting for their friends to show up. They went shopping without Martha and Patricia. And Martha and Patricia were so confused that they decided to go back home."

   Question: **"What should Martha and Patricia have done when they first became confused?"**

3. **Identify the Skill Components:** List these on the board or on sentence strips.

   1. Decide if you need help.
   2. Think about and list some consequences of *not* asking for help.
   3. Find the right person to help you and ask that person for help.
   4. Role play the situation in your mind or with a friend before you actually follow through.

22

    5. Follow through on their suggestions.

    6. Create new friendships by asking for help.

4. ***Model the Skill:*** Individual class members will name times when they needed help. The teacher will guide the class through the steps in the skill components as a means of deciding when and how to ask for help.

5. ***Behavioral Rehearsal:***

    A. *Selection:* Teacher selects ten volunteers to role play.

    B. *Role Plays:*

        (1) The class will role play the story presented in the introduction. In addition to the four major roles, others are needed to portray those who could have helped but weren't asked (e.g., bus driver, other passengers, bus line employee in the information booth, etc.).

        (2) Volunteers will role play this situation: Martha's parents just got a divorce. Her friends at school have noticed the change in her. She hardly ever talks to them, and even seems angry when they try to talk to her. Martha's teachers noticed that her grades are dropping, but she won't discuss this. Martha has stopped communicating with her parents, except when absolutely necessary.

    C. *Completion:* After the role play, reinforce correct behavior, identify inappropriate behavior, and reenact role play with corrections. If there are no corrections, role play is complete.

    D. *Reinforcers:* Teacher and peers should acknowledge correct behavior with verbal praise. Reinforcement will also be provided by acknowledging improvement in social and academic areas because the student has learned to ask for help when needed.

    E. *Discussion:* Critique not only how the role players focused on the skills but how well the audience critiqued the role playing situation.

6. ***Practice:*** Have students complete the following worksheet, "Speak Up!," listing the names of people who could help them in a problem situation.

7. ***Independent Use:*** Hand out copies of the worksheet entitled "Asking for Help" and direct students to do as follows:

    "Pick a person in your family who would be the one you would most likely ask for help. Think of something they could help you with and write a letter to that person asking for help. Give the letter to the teacher at the end of the week."

8. ***Continuation:*** Teacher will point out that people who learn to ask for help when needed will not feel inadequate. They will feel more confident and become more skillful and informed. Hopefully, new friendships will be formed and old ones strengthened, since others appreciate being recognized and consulted.

Name _____   Date _____

SPEAK UP!

WE CAN'T READ YOUR MIND!

Make a list of the people who could help you when you have questions or problems.

_____

_____

_____

_____

_____

_____

_____

_____

_____

_____

_____

_____

_____

Name _____ Date _____

ASKING FOR HELP - LETTER

In my family, I go to _____
when I have a problem.

Write a letter to that person asking for help with a question or a problem.

Dear _____,

_____

_____

_____

_____

_____

_____

_____

_____

_____

_____

_____

_____

_____

_____

USING PERSUASION   Lesson 7

SOCIAL SKILL
Convincing Others to Do Right

Behavioral Objective: The student will understand that trying to convince others to do the right thing is always an appropriate and commendable behavior.

Directed Lesson:

1. **Establish the Need:** Convincing other students to do the right thing is commendable. At home or in school, it helps everyone achieve a more harmonious existence. Discuss with the students what would happen if everyone tried to convince others to do the right thing. Their lives would be more pleasant, and it would create a safer environment for all of us.

2. **Introduction:** Teacher will ask the following questions for an open discussion:

   ▶ What strategies can you use for completing homework assignments?

   ▶ Where can you find a quiet location so that you can concentrate on your homework and assignments?

   ▶ What do you need to do to ensure that you get enough sleep?

   ▶ If you could set one new goal for yourself today, what would it be?

3. **Identify the Skill Components:** Write the following skill components on the board or on sentence strips.

   1. Decide why you want to convince someone to do right.
   2. Approach the person in a friendly way.
   3. Tell the other person what your idea is.
   4. Ask the other person what their opinion is about what you said.
   5. Explain to them why your suggestion is a good idea.
   6. Ask the other person to think about what you have said.

4. **Model the Skill:** Ask the students to role play a student who is in need of changing his behavior. He will be approached by the teacher. The teacher will pretend to be a student. The teacher will use the six skill components to try to convince the student to behave in class. When this is done, ask the students to explain step-by-step what the teacher did.

5. **Behavioral Rehearsal:**

   A. *Selection:* Ask for volunteers.

   B. *Role Play:* Ask the groups to role play situations such as getting to class on time, doing homework, going to school, getting enough sleep, saying "No" to drugs and sex.

Have one student from each group try to convince the other student to follow his/her advice. The student should try to use the six skill components. The class will critique each situation.

C. *Completion:* After each role play, the teacher will reinforce correct behavior and identify inappropriate behaviors. The students may do the role play over again if there was anything wrong. If it was correct, the role play is complete.

D. *Reinforcers:* Both the teacher and the class should reinforce correct behavior with verbal praise.

E. *Discussion:* The students and teacher will discuss each situation and verbally evaluate the behaviors.

6. **Practice:** Give each student a copy of the two-page worksheet, "Convincing Others (to Do Right)," which presents a story situation that is incomplete. The students' assignment will be twofold: (1) to complete the story (fill in the blanks), and (2) state what is different about the two boys during the last encounter two months after the incident. Also write down what you think is the relationship between the boys two months after the car incident.

7. **Independent Use:** The students will complete the worksheet entitled "Interview Form" at home. They will interview a family member or a friend to ask if they have ever tried to convince someone (a co-worker, relative, friend) to do the "right thing." The students will write the person's response on the worksheet, then ask the person to check over what has been written and sign the form at the bottom if it is correct.

8. **Continuation:** Teacher can reinforce this skill every time someone demonstrates inappropriate behavior. The teacher can say, "Perhaps someone would like to try to convince 'Billy' that appropriate behavior is the right thing to do."

Name _____ Date _____

CONVINCING OTHERS TO DO RIGHT

Directions: Complete the story by filling in the blanks and answering the questions.

Two boys by the names of James and Vincent are best friends.

They do everything together. They started _____
together in the first grade. They have remained together all the way into
seventh grade. They even have some _____
together. They play _____ together, and they like
the same _____. If Vincent likes a girl, then James
likes her too. If James dislikes his _____ teacher,
then Vincent dislikes him too.

One day James and Vincent are walking down the street. They see a brand-new
_____ sitting on the corner. The motor is run-
ning, the doors are unlocked, and of course the _____ are in
the ignition. Vincent screams with joy and says, "Oh, boy _____
_____." James says "No way." Using the six skill components,
explain what James will say next.

1. _____

2. _____

3. _____

4. _____

5. _____

6. _____

Name _____ Date _____

CONVINCING OTHERS TO DO RIGHT
(Continued)

James is very persuasive and convinces Vincent not to steal the car. They continue walking to the store. When they come out of the store, they see their friend Carlos. He is with the police. His hands are _____ behind his back. Carlos is being led to a police _____. He is screaming at the police. "The keys were in it. It isn't my fault. I _____." Vincent and James are shocked. Carlos has been arrested for stealing a car—the same car Vincent wanted to joy _____ in a few minutes ago. Vincent turns to James and says "_____
_____."

Two months later, Carlos is released from the detention home. James and Vincent run into him on the street. Explain how each one feels now.

1. James_____
   _____
   _____

2. Vincent_____
   _____
   _____

3. Carlos_____
   _____
   _____

Name _____ Date _____

INTERVIEW FORM

Use this form to interview a family member or friend.

1. Have you ever convinced someone to do the right thing? Please describe the incident when you tried.

2. Were you successful?

3. What happened later?

4. May I have your permission to share this information with my classmates?

YES   NO   ONLY IF.....

SOCIAL SKILL
Convincing Someone to Do the Right Thing

Behavioral Objective: The student will understand that trying to convince someone else to do the right thing is always an appropriate and commendable behavior. It helps both people to excel.

Directed Lesson:

1. ***Establish the Need:*** Convincing other students to do the right thing is a commendable thing. At home or in school, it helps everyone achieve a more harmonious existence. Discuss with the students what would happen if everyone tried to convince others to do the right thing. Then their life (at home, at school, and in the community) would be more pleasant. It would also create a safer environment for everyone.

2. ***Introduction:*** Teacher will ask the following questions for class discussion:

    ▶ If you know a particular behavior is right, how can you convince someone to change?

    ▶ How can you convince someone that outcomes are the logical consequences of choices made in the beginning (inputs)?

    ▶ What strategies do you find successful, when convincing *yourself* to do what's right to do?

    "Tara was Neisha's friend. Tara couldn't believe that Neisha was interested in such a sleeze as Vernon. Tara was a very nice girl. She thought to tell Neisha that she was making a big mistake. Tara knew that Neisha shouldn't have anything to do with Vernon.
    "Should Tara say anything? How can she get started?"

3. ***Identify the Skill Components:*** List the following skill components on the board or on sentence strips.

    1. Decide what is right and what is wrong.
    2. Decide why you want to convince someone to do right.
    3. Approach the person in a friendly manner.
    4. Tell the other person what your idea is, be positive and forceful.
    5. Ask the other person what their opinion is about what you've said.
    6. Explain to them that the consequences of their actions can last forever. Keep explaining even if opposed.
    7. Ask the other person to think about what you have said.
    8. Be persistent—don't quit, keep trying. Explain that consequences should always be considered before acting.

4. ***Model the Skill:*** The teacher begins by saying, **"Have you ever tried to tell someone that they are making a mistake?"** The teacher then relates a personal story to the students about the time he/she tried to convince a student to do the right thing.

    Here are some examples:

    ▶ a student who is preparing to cheat on a test in another class
    ▶ a friend who wanted to buy or sell drugs

    The teacher should then use the skill components in the story introduction to show how he or she handled the situation.

5. ***Behavioral Rehearsal:***

    A. *Selection:* Ask for volunteers. Place the students in pairs.

    B. *Role Play:* Have one student in each pair try to convince the other student to follow their advice. The students should try to be as convincing as possible and try to use the skill components.

        Here are several role play situations:

        -   convince a friend not to fight
        -   convince a friend to go to school on time every day
        -   convince a friend not to have sex
        -   convince a friend not to do drugs

        Let the class think of some situations on their own.

    C. *Completion:* After each role play, the teacher should reinforce the correct behavior and identify inappropriate behaviors. The students should repeat the role play with the new corrections. If it was good and correct, the role play is complete.

    D. *Reinforcers:* The class should applaud all role plays. Verbal praise from both the teacher and the class is essential.

    E. *Discussion:* The students and teacher will discuss each role play. The criteria for judgment should be based on the skill components. The class will verbally evaluate the behaviors in each role play. If there is no resolution, it may be unnecessary to cover all eight skill components.

6. ***Practice:*** The students will complete the worksheet "Why Should You Convince Someone to Do Right?" consisting of two columns. Column I has five negative actions. Column II has 25 consequences for these actions. The students are to find as many consequences for the actions as possible. This can lead to a discussion of each inappropriate (wrong) action. The idea is that someone can avoid these consequences if you can convince them to do the right thing.

7. ***Independent Use:*** The students will be given the worksheet entitled "How Much Will It Cost?" to take home. This worksheet lists ten items suggesting ten situations. The students are to find the cost of each item. They can go anywhere to obtain this information. Next, they should write down the situation and consequences suggested by each item.

8. ***Continuation:*** The teacher can reinforce this skill each time someone demonstrates inappropriate behavior. The teacher can say, "Perhaps someone would like to try to convince the others that appropriate behavior is the right thing to do and can save money."

Name _____ Date _____

WHY SHOULD YOU CONVINCE SOMEONE TO DO RIGHT?

Directions: Read the actions and consequences below. Then, in the rectangle provided under each topic in Column I, write the numbers from Column II that could be a consequence of that action. Discuss.

COLUMN I - ACTION

A. The use of drugs leads to:

B. Sex leads to:

C. Gang membership leads to:

D. Cheating leads to:

E. Stealing leads to:

COLUMN II - CONSEQUENCE

1. Death
2. Jail
3. Poor grades
4. No future
5. School punishment
6. No job
7. Being poor
8. Failing a grade
9. Physical pain
10. Arrest
11. No money
12. Ill health
13. Pregnancy
14. Criminal record
15. New unwanted responsibility
16. Not graduating
17. Disease
18. Bad reputation

Extra money is need for:

19. Baby food
20. Doctor bills
21. Baby clothes
22. Day care
23. Bail
24. Medicine
25. More drugs

Name _____ Date _____

HOW MUCH WILL IT COST?

Directions: How much do the items or activities listed below cost? Who can you ask or where can you telephone to find out? List the ESTIMATED cost first, then the ACTUAL cost next to it. How close were you?

	ESTIMATE	ACTUAL
1. A jar of baby food	_____	_____
2. An x-ray of your arm	_____	_____
3. One bottle of aspirin tablets	_____	_____
4. A box of baby diapers	_____	_____
5. A lawyer's consultation fee	_____	_____
6. A phone call from the police station	_____	_____
7. A visit to a pediatrician	_____	_____
8. Court cost for traffic ticket	_____	_____
9. A night's stay in a hospital	_____	_____
10. An emergency room visit	_____	_____

How much did you estimate? $_____

What is the actual cost? $_____

SOCIAL SKILL
Knowing Your Feelings

Behavioral Objective: Students will be able to identify, label with precision, and accept their own feelings during both positive and negative experiences.

Directed Lesson:

1. ***Establish the Need:*** Students need to be aware that all real feelings are legitimate; that they are caused by a combination of experiences and their own interpretations of those experiences; and that "owning" genuine feelings opens the door to personal growth.

2. ***Introduction:*** Tell the following story:

   "Today Bill's class is going on a field trip, and just this morning, Bill woke up late. His mother scolded him for his messy room, for getting up late, and for spilling milk at breakfast. On the way to school, he got into a fight with his best friend. He arrived in homeroom late, and hoped the teacher wouldn't notice. Wrong! When permission slips were being collected, Bill suddenly realized that his was on the table at home. He asked the teacher if he could call home to get permission. The teacher's frown was like a loud silent 'No!' but after a few minutes she agreed."

   Ask the class to identify feelings at various points in the story. Then ask the class to name any additional feelings they know about and identify the listed feelings as positive ("good") or negative ("bad").

3. ***Identify the Skill Components:*** List the following skill components on the board or on sentence strips.

   1. Identify what happens in your body when you have "feelings."
   2. Identify what events happened just before the feeling occurred.
   3. Identify what previous events had an effect on the feeling.
   4. Identify the understandings or interpretations you brought to the event.
   5. Label the feeling as accurately as possible (e.g., joyful, happy, pleased, satisfied, angry, resentful, irritated, furious).

4. ***Model the Skill:*** Teacher invites a student to make a personal remark (physical appearance, age, personality) to or about the teacher. The teacher then responds to the student's remark by specifically naming the feeling he/she got because of the remark.

5.   *Behavioral Rehearsal:*

   A. *Selection:* Teacher selects students in groups of four to role play.

   B. *Role Play:* The scenario: A teacher returns tests to two students. One, who usually has received F's and D's, has the highest grade on this test. Another, a friend of the first, usually leads the class but failed this test. A third student, not in the same class, is a good friend of both. The two interact with each other, with the teacher, and with their mutual friend. A second group is assigned to observe the individuals in the role play to identify and label expected feelings and displayed feelings.

   C. *Completion:* After each role play, reinforce correct behavior, identify inappropriate behaviors, and reenact role play with correction. If there are no corrections, role play is complete.

   D. *Reinforcers:* Give positive verbal and nonverbal praise (smile, pat on the back).

   E. *Discussion:* Discuss the legitimacy of the feelings identified in the role play and the appropriateness of the resulting behavior. Lead the class in identifying other feelings which could also be aroused in this and similar occurrences. Stress that labels of positive and negative feelings are related to the appropriateness and effectiveness of resulting behavior.

6.   *Practice:* Distribute copies of the worksheet entitled "Your Feelings in Real Life." Compare the results as time permits. Students can finish the worksheet at home and return it to the teacher.

7.   *Independent Use:* Students will take copies of the worksheet entitled "A Diary of My Feelings" home to record events, feelings, behaviors, and results.

8.   *Continuation:* Teacher should continue pointing out the need for this skill as related situations arise.

Name _____ Date _____

YOUR FEELINGS IN REAL LIFE

Event: What happened?	Expected Feeling(s) (more than one?)	"Good" or "Bad"	"What would you do?" (choice of behavior)	Results: What next?
Your lunch card or money is stolen.				
Someone ratted to a teacher about something you did.				
You have been dared into a fight you think you'll *lose*.				
You have been dared into a fight you think you'll *win*.				
You just had a haircut or perm you hate and don't want to show.				
Your grandfather died and your family doesn't seem to care.				
Adults are always comparing you with a brother/sister.				

Name _____ Date _____

A DIARY OF MY FEELINGS

Directions: In the boxes below, record three things that happened to you. How did you feel? How did you act? How did it work out? Discuss with classmates.

What Happened (Event)	How I Felt (Feeling)	What I Did (Behavior)	How It Worked (Result)
1.			
2.			
3.			

SOCIAL SKILL

Recognizing and Accepting Your Feelings

Behavioral Objective: Students will be capable of recognizing, identifying, and accepting their feelings in both positive and negative situations.

Directed Lesson:

1. **Establish the Need:** Students need to recognize the legitimacy of feelings and to understand that they are caused by a combination of circumstances. They must also be able to recognize those causes that make them feel a certain way.

2. **Introduction:** Tell the following story to the class:

    "Last night Frank was at his girlfriend Carla's house. Her parents were upstairs watching TV, and Frank and Carla were in the basement listening to music. Carla's parents had a rule about how late her company could stay. Frank usually wanted to stay later, but her parents were insistent, and Frank had to leave. When they politely told Frank it was time to go home, he wouldn't go. He was not prepared for their reaction. They ordered him out of the house—never to return. He tried to apologize, but they wouldn't listen. The next morning Frank tried to call Carla on the phone. Her parents told him not to call back. When he approached her at school, Carla looked as if she had been crying. She refused to look at him, much less talk to him."

    Ask the students about how Frank felt, how Carla felt, and how Carla's parents felt when Frank directly challenged their authority in their home. What is the lesson that Frank needs to learn? What is the lesson the parents should learn? Should they accept an apology?

3. **Identify the Skill Components:** List the following skill components on the board before class:

    1. Recognize that feelings are a natural response to experience.
    2. Feelings may be positive or negative.
    3. Accept feelings as a physical happening.
    4. Identify feelings that are enjoyable.
    5. Identify feelings of withdrawal.
    6. Recognize the causes of feelings.
    7. Discriminate between causes of feelings that can be changed and cannot be changed.
    8. Accept feelings you cannot change.
    9. Adjust feelings accordingly.

4. ***Model the Skill:*** Teacher invites a student to join in one or more of the following scenes. The teacher acts out the feeling, then labels it:

   ▶ student unfairly accuses the teacher of stealing a pencil

   ▶ teacher calls the student by the wrong name; student gets angry; teacher is embarrassed

   ▶ student tells teacher "You have favorite students in class."

5. ***Behavioral Rehearsal:***

   A. *Selection:* Teacher divides the class into groups of four to enact as many of the role plays as time and size of class allow.

   B. *Role Play:* Two students role play a scene from the story, then the others identify the feelings and the causes.

   Examples for role play:

   - Role play Carla's parents discussing Frank before the incident/after the incident.
   - Role play Carla and her parents talking after Frank left the house.
   - Role play Frank talking to a friend about the incident.
   - Role play the appropriate behavior when you're a guest in someone's home.

   C. *Completion:* After each role play, reinforce the correct behavior, identify inappropriate behaviors, and reenact the role play with corrections. If there are no corrections, the role play is complete.

   D. *Reinforcers:* Use verbal and nonverbal praise (specific).

   E. *Discussion:* Discuss the role play and the kinds of feelings evoked. Help students discover any additional feelings which might be expected in these and similar situations. Encourage comments as to the kind and degree of control the persons in the role plays had or didn't have over their feelings.

6. ***Practice:*** Hand out copies of the worksheet "What's the Feeling?" for students to complete and return.

7. ***Independent Use:*** Have students take a copy of the worksheet from the previous lesson, "A Diary of My Feelings," home to record events, feelings, behaviors, and results.

8. ***Continuation:*** Teacher should continue to point out the need for this skill as related situations arise.

Name _____ Date _____

WHAT'S THE FEELING?

Directions: From the following list of words, choose the feeling that matches the situation in each of the eight situations described below. Write the word you have chosen on the line following the situation.

joy
disappointment
excitement   happiness
anger   embarrassment   fear   sadness
anxiety   frustration

1. You have just been elected president of the student council.

   _____

2. You didn't receive a birthday gift you really wanted.

   _____

3. Your favorite entertainer is in town. You just received free concert tickets.

   _____

4. Your family accused you unjustly of stealing $100.00.

   _____

5. Your favorite uncle has been in an accident.

   _____

6. You forgot your lines in the school play.

   _____

7. No matter how hard you try, you can't fix your bicycle.

   _____

8. John the "big" bully is looking for you.

   _____

DEALING WITH FEELINGS   Lesson 11

SOCIAL SKILL
Expressing Your Feelings

Behavioral Objective: Students will interpret their feelings, choose ways to deal with them, and recognize comparable feelings in others.

Directed Lesson:

1. ***Establish the Need:*** All feelings are legitimate. Students need to learn how to express their feelings. They need to choose appropriate behaviors for dealing with these feelings.

2. ***Introduction:*** Refer to TV program episodes within the previous two weeks having to do with family situations and/or social situations. After summarizing the episode to remind those who have seen it and inform those who have not, elicit responses as to feelings involved, expressions, interaction, behavior choices, and consequences. (Movies seen recently by many of the students can be used as well.) NOTE: Time and equipment permitting, a brief video-taped episode can be used for this purpose.

3. ***Identify the Skill Components:*** Write the following skill components on the board or on sentence strips.

   1. Recognize what happens when you experience internal feelings.
   2. Express what event happened just before the feelings occurred.
   3. What understanding did you bring to the event by expressing your feelings?
   4. Label the feeling as accurately as possible, for instance, angry, resentful, irritated, furious, joyful, happy, pleased, and satisfied.
   5. Communicate (verbally and nonverbally) the feeling to others.
   6. Recognize and identify comparable feelings in others.
   7. Choose appropriate behaviors to deal with feelings, your own and others.

4. ***Model the Skill:*** Select a situation from one of the TV shows or movies in which two characters have expressed strong feelings. Teacher and a student will role play. Teacher will show understanding of the student's feelings and will calmly deal with them.

5. ***Behavioral Rehearsal:***

   A. *Selection:* Teacher selects enough students for three role plays.

   B. *Role Play:* An event from one of the TV programs or movies is role played by the first group. The second and third groups reenact the same event with a significant change in the assigned feelings/behavior (e.g., anger to fear, joy to jealousy, enthusiasm to boredom, excitement to disappointment).

C. *Completion:* After each role play, reinforce correct behavior, identify inappropriate behavior, and reenact role play with corrections. If there are no corrections, role play is complete.

D. *Reinforcers:* Reinforce appropriate behavior with verbal and nonverbal praise (specific) and tangible rewards.

E. *Discussion:* Discuss the feelings identified in the role play. Encourage students to suggest alternate behaviors. Identify the feelings that could be aroused in self and others.

6. **Practice:** Hand out copies of the following word search puzzle for students to complete.

7. **Independent Use:** Give students copies of the worksheet entitled "Expressing Your Feelings" as a homework assignment. Note that more than one feeling can be perceived, that many different kinds of events might have caused the perceived feeling, and that there can be a wide diversity of causes and results.

8. **Continuation:** Teacher should continue pointing out the need for this skill as related situations arise.

Name _____ Date _____

WORD SEARCH

Directions: Read the words in the word bank below. Then find them on the grid, and draw a circle around them. Words can be found horizontally, vertically, diagonally, forward, and backward.

```
M A D E R O B R L
A B A N D O N E D
N E R V O U S A D
G T Z D G T I G Y
R R D L A R L E X
Y A Y V O A L R E
A Y N A Z G Y O S
G E V I L E B A D
X D I V I D E D S
```

WORD BANK

abandoned	odd	angry		sexy
nervous	silly	bored		mad
betrayed	divided	zany	sad	ugly
eager	evil	outraged		gay

Name _____ Date _____

EXPRESSING YOUR FEELINGS

Directions: Study the face. Record the feeling. Then write (1) What caused the feeling, and (2) How do you respond?

What You See	Cause of Feeling?	Response to Feeling
		1. 2.
		1. 2.
		1. 2.
		1. 2.

SOCIAL SKILL

Expressing Empathy for Others

Behavioral Objective: Students will identify and accept their own feelings and choose clear verbal and nonverbal ways of expressing these feelings. Students will identify and accept the feelings of others and use situational and behavioral clues to access those feelings.

Directed Lesson:

1.   **Establish the Need:** Students need to develop a better understanding of their feelings and the feelings of others, and the effects feelings have on motivating their own behavior and that of others.

2.   **Introduction:** Tell the following story:

> **"Matt didn't want to go to social studies, but he couldn't quite figure out why. He did like the teacher, but somehow he didn't like the class. The teacher had scheduled a test today, and Matt wasn't ready. He knew where there was an empty room. No one ever went there, so he went. Halfway through the period Matt smelled smoke, looked in the next room, and discovered a fire! Should he report it? Ignore it? He ran and told the first teacher he saw that there was a fire, thus getting help in time to put out the fire. Matt was told to report to the principal's office. The question the principal faced: Should he talk to Matt, the hero, who discovered the fire, or to Matt, the class cutter, or to both identities?"**

Ask the class to identify the feelings of Matt, the teacher, and the principal. Suggest to speak about the feelings as the parties in the story might express them.

3.   **Identifying the Skill Components:** Write the following skill components on the board or on sentence strips.

    1.   Identify your own feeling (fearful, confused, elated, etc.).
    2.   Distinguish the intensity of the feeling (sad, furious, happy, ecstatic).
    3.   Decide whether communicating the feeling will help.
    4.   Communicate the feeling (if necessary).
    5.   Choose words and applicable behaviors.
    6.   Be alert to others' feelings.
    7.   Accept others' feelings.
    8.   Express your acceptance.

4.   **Model the Skill:** Using the story from the introduction: Teacher selects a student to represent Matt and he/she role plays the principal. The teacher invites the student to express Matt's feelings, assisting the student in the expression of his feelings.

5.   **Behavioral Rehearsal:**

  A. *Selection:* Choose groups of two for role play.

  B. *Role Play:* Present each group with one of the following situations. Two students role play the situation, giving expression to their feelings.

    – A student's mother bought two lottery tickets, one for herself and one for a friend. The friend's ticket won $100,000.

    – Bart has just been invited to take sky-diving lessons, including his first jump. He's afraid of heights. He talks it over with a friend, who wishes he could go instead.

  C. *Completion:* After each role play, reinforce correct behavior, identify inappropriate behaviors, and reenact role play with corrections. If there are no corrections, role play is complete.

  D. *Reinforcers:* Use verbal and nonverbal praise (specific).

  E. *Discussion:* Discuss the feelings expressed in the story and in the role plays. Emphasize the reality of different and even contradictory feelings resulting from differing perceptions and interpretations. Also discuss the need for sensitivity to the feelings of others, as they may be different from one's own.

6.   **Practice:** Hand out copies of the following worksheet, "Those Feelings Are Ba-a-ack!" Fill out different feelings that may be evoked in similar situations. Have students complete the worksheet in class.

7.   **Independent Use:** Before distributing the worksheet "Express Your Feelings," remind the students that this is not an easy task they will be doing, and that sometimes expressing feelings can be difficult, but necessary.

8.   **Continuation:** The teacher should continue pointing out the need for this skill as related situations arise.

Name _____ Date _____

THOSE FEELINGS ARE BA-A-ACK!

Directions: What might someone be feeling when they demonstrate each of the following behaviors? Use the word or words from the "FEELINGS BOX" below, and write them on the lines. There is more than one correct answer.

FEELINGS

1. **They stomp their feet** ------------- ----------- -----------

2. **Their eyes are filled with tears** _____ _____ _____

3. **They fall asleep in class** _____ _____ _____

4. **They are laughing** ------------- ------------- -------------

5. **They are not picked to be on a team** _____ _____ _____

6. **They are called names** _____ _____ _____

7. **They are laughed at** _____ _____ _____

8. **They don't ask a question** _____ _____ _____

9. **They are a new student** _____ _____ _____

10. **They keep looking at their watch** _____ _____ _____

11. **They are punished unjustly** _____ _____ _____

12. **They can't seem to do anything right** _____ _____ _____

FEELINGS BOX:

nervous	bad mood	embarrassed	disappointment
sadness	fear	worry	excitement
anger	happiness	frustration	joy

Name _____ Date _____

EXPRESS YOUR FEELINGS!

Directions: Eight different feelings are listed in the column below. Think of a situation that might cause each feeling, and write the cause in the second column. Next, think of how you might express the feeling to others and write this in the third column.

FEELING	CAUSE	EXPRESSION
1. Sadness	_ _ _ _ _ _ _ _ _ _ _	_ _ _ _ _ _ _ _ _ _ _
	_ _ _ _ _ _ _ _ _ _ _	_ _ _ _ _ _ _ _ _ _ _
2. Frustration	_ _ _ _ _ _ _ _ _ _ _	_ _ _ _ _ _ _ _ _ _ _
	_ _ _ _ _ _ _ _ _ _ _	_ _ _ _ _ _ _ _ _ _ _
3. Worry	_ _ _ _ _ _ _ _ _ _ _	_ _ _ _ _ _ _ _ _ _ _
	_ _ _ _ _ _ _ _ _ _ _	_ _ _ _ _ _ _ _ _ _ _
4. Joy	_ _ _ _ _ _ _ _ _ _ _	_ _ _ _ _ _ _ _ _ _ _
	_ _ _ _ _ _ _ _ _ _ _	_ _ _ _ _ _ _ _ _ _ _
5. Excitement	_ _ _ _ _ _ _ _ _ _ _	_ _ _ _ _ _ _ _ _ _ _
	_ _ _ _ _ _ _ _ _ _ _	_ _ _ _ _ _ _ _ _ _ _
6. Embarrassed	_ _ _ _ _ _ _ _ _ _ _	_ _ _ _ _ _ _ _ _ _ _
	_ _ _ _ _ _ _ _ _ _ _	_ _ _ _ _ _ _ _ _ _ _
7. Anger	_ _ _ _ _ _ _ _ _ _ _	_ _ _ _ _ _ _ _ _ _ _
	_ _ _ _ _ _ _ _ _ _ _	_ _ _ _ _ _ _ _ _ _ _
8. Happiness	_ _ _ _ _ _ _ _ _ _ _	_ _ _ _ _ _ _ _ _ _ _
	_ _ _ _ _ _ _ _ _ _ _	_ _ _ _ _ _ _ _ _ _ _

SOCIAL SKILL
Expressing Affection

Behavioral Objective: The students will be able to identify and express appropriate feelings toward others. The students will be capable of recognizing and appreciating the positive feeling of others toward themselves.

Directed Lesson:

1. **Establish the Need:** Many students have not internalized the idea that "the best way to have a friend is to be a friend." They will be more apt to form friendships when they learn, not only how to recognize their own feelings, but how to express them.

2. **Introduction:** Ask members of the class to name some well-known persons. (They can be people from entertainment, sports, politics, etc.) Choose one of the persons named, and have the class make a list of positive comments about that person. Next, list some negative comments about the person. Discuss how we can have opposite responses about the same person. Encourage students to do the same thing with their own personal traits as well as those of their acquaintances and friends.

3. **Identify the Skill Components:** List the following skill components on the board before class.

   1. Decide if you have any good feelings about the other person(s).
   2. Determine the exact good feeling(s) you have.
   3. Identify the attribute(s) you have noticed that brought about the good feeling(s).
   4. Decide whether the other person(s) would like to know about your feeling(s).
   5. Choose the best way to express your feeling(s) in a friendly and non-demanding way.
   6. Remember how *you* feel when someone lets you know something good about yourself.
   7. Realize that if you follow the skill steps listed above, others will notice something good about you.

4. **Model the Skill:** Teacher offers approving comments such as emphasizing and labeling responsive feelings of participating students during the Introduction ("You noticed something I didn't notice; thank you.") and, as appropriate, about students' manner or appearance ("That's a very attractive blouse"). Some may be mildly embarrassed by being singled out, but most are likely to be pleased that their efforts, manner, or appearance are appreciated.

5. **Behavioral Rehearsal:**

   A. *Selection:* Teacher arranges students in pairs (an odd student can join a pair). Pairs are coupled into groups of four.

B. *Role Play:* In pairs, students take turns telling each other what one thing about themselves they wish other people would notice. Pairs then join in groups of four, and each takes a turn expressing a positive comment and feeling about his/her partner. As time permits, one or more students from each group repeats the positive comments and feelings to the entire class. *NOTE:* If any student feels uncomfortable about personal exposure, participants can alternatively represent themselves as some imaginary or real person and make up an attribute not real but to be noticed.

C. *Completion:* After each group reports, reinforce correct comments and behavior, identify inappropriate comments and behavior, and repeat the role play with corrections. If there are no corrections, role play is complete.

D. *Reinforcers:* Give verbal and nonverbal praise (specific) for correct behavior.

E. *Discussion:* Discuss the role plays. Students should be encouraged to express their feelings in response to hearing positive descriptions and expressions of positive feelings spoken by others about themselves. What would it feel like to be the only one about whom such feelings were expressed?—about whom no such feelings were expressed?

6. ***Practice:*** Give students copies of the following worksheet entitled "Scramble Sheet" and the accompanying answer key page, and tell them to unscramble the words of affection (you may want to retain the answer key until most students have finished).

7. ***Independent Use:*** Send home the worksheet "How Do You Do, _____" and ask students to complete it and bring it back to class for discussion at a certain date.

8. ***Continuation:*** Teacher should continue pointing out the need for this skill as related situations arise.

Name _____ Date _____

SCRAMBLE SHEET

Directions: Below are 15 scrambled words that are used to express affection. How many can you find? Write them on the line.

1. glovni   _____

2. plantsea   _____

3. donerlufw   _____

4. petruar   _____

5. soyjou   _____

6. fictonfateea   _____

7. tinfataued   _____

8. satdiefis   _____

9. vaciousvi   _____

10. oyenijgn   _____

11. satedcinfa   _____

12. facepeul   _____

13. talviyti   _____

14. tighledde   _____

15. stactiec   _____

Stuck?   See Answer Key.

SCRAMBLE SHEET ANSWER KEY

ANSWERS:

joyous
loving
pleasant
wonderful
fascinated
satisfied
ecstatic
vivacious
vitality
delighted
infatuated
affectionate
rapture
enjoying
peaceful

OOPS!
Answers are in Scrambled order.
Need more help?

Clues: 5   1   2   3   11   8   15   9   13

14   7   6   4   10   12

Name _____   Date _____

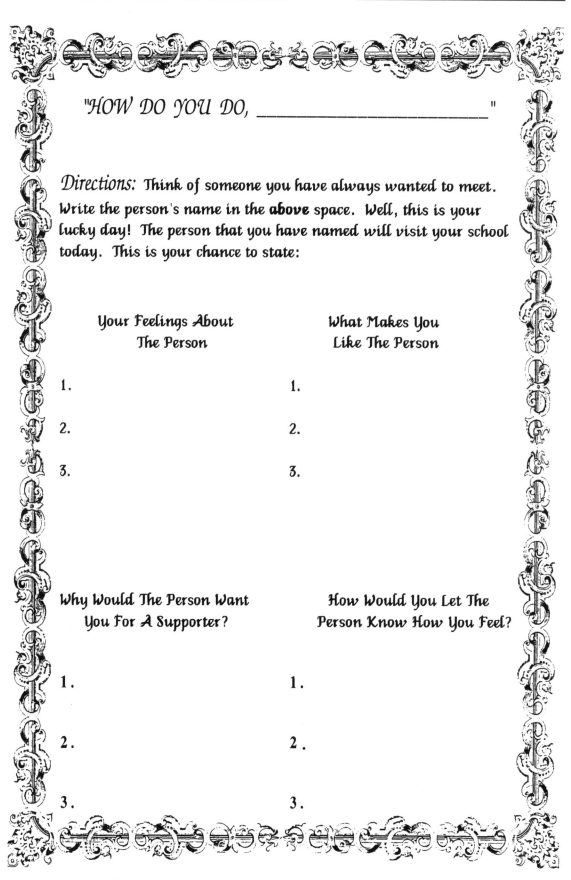

"HOW DO YOU DO, _____"

Directions: Think of someone you have always wanted to meet. Write the person's name in the **above** space. Well, this is your lucky day! The person that you have named will visit your school today. This is your chance to state:

Your Feelings About The Person	What Makes You Like The Person
1.	1.
2.	2.
3.	3.

Why Would The Person Want You For A Supporter?	How Would You Let The Person Know How You Feel?
1.	1.
2.	2.
3.	3.

SOCIAL SKILL
Expressing Affection

Behavioral Objective: The students will be able to identify and express appropriate feelings toward others. The students will be capable of recognizing and appreciating the positive feeling of others toward themselves.

Directed Lesson:

1. **Establish the Need:** Students need to widen their understanding of affection to include more than just the normal circle of friends. They need to discover the wealth of assets in the abilities, personalities, and accomplishments of a wide range of persons with whom they may have contact. To express positive attitudes and feelings is to open the door to potential relationships and opportunities that otherwise might have remained closed.

2. **Introduction:** Ask the following questions. Encourage any responses students may offer, but allow a few moments for reflection even if no verbal responses are given:

    ❱ How do you feel when someone criticizes you unfairly?

    ❱ How do you feel when the criticism is deserved?

    ❱ What does it feel like to be praised when you don't deserve it?

    ❱ When you do deserve it?

    ❱ What is the difference between flattery and a sincere compliment?

3. **Identify the Skill Components:** Write the following skill components on the board or on sentence strips.

    1. Identify something positive about the other person(s).
    2. Identify your positive feeling(s) about the person(s).
    3. Decide if the person(s) will benefit by knowing your feelings.
    4. Choose a time and place for expressing feeling(s).
    5. Express your feelings appropriately.
    6. Be sincere.
    7. Anticipate response: How does the other person feel?
    8. Accept the expressions from others without embarrassment.

4. **Model the Skill:** Teacher offers sincere positive comments about a number of students. These can be about appearance, manner, dress, scholarship, etc. Emphasize the relationship between the skill components and positive comments about others.

5. *Behavioral Rehearsal:*

A. *Selection:* Divide the class into groups of three.

B. *Role Play:* Give the groups up to 5 minutes (as time permits) to talk with each other and to ask and answer any questions needed for the assignment.

In turn, each member of the group of three verbally expresses positive, favorable, affectionate feelings to each of the other two that he/she *believes to be true.*

C. *Completion:* After each role play, reinforce correct behavior, identify inappropriate behaviors, and reenact role play with corrections. If there are no corrections, role play is complete.

D. *Reinforcers:* Use verbal and nonverbal praise (specific).

E. *Discussion*: Students evaluate the role play for appropriate and inappropriate behaviors and make corrections, if needed. Use one or more of the following questions as discussion starters:

- Why do many people find expressing affection difficult?

- How can you appropriately express gratitude to someone who has done a favor for you? Give examples of the words and phrases that can be used.

- When someone gives you a compliment, give examples of how you can respond.

6. *Practice:* Hand out the worksheet "Words of Affection" for students to fill in the blanks with affectionate words. If time permits, connotations of some of the words can be explored.

7. *Independent Usage:* Give students copies of the worksheet "Affection" to take home and complete before sharing it with parents. They can then bring the worksheet back to class and share it with the teacher and their classmates.

8. *Continuation:* Teacher should continue pointing out the need for this skill as related situations arise.

Name _____ Date _____

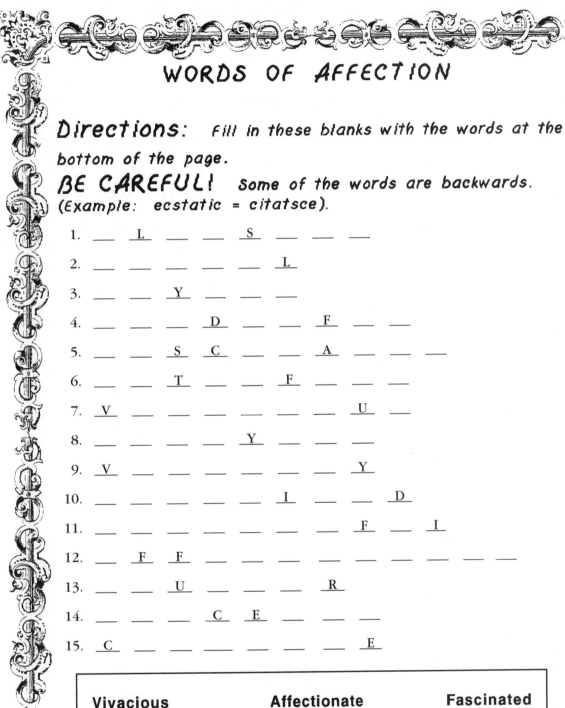

WORDS OF AFFECTION

Directions: *Fill in these blanks with the words at the bottom of the page.*
BE CAREFUL! *Some of the words are backwards.*
(Example: ecstatic = citatsce).

1. __ L __ __ S __ __ __

2. __ __ __ __ __ L

3. __ __ Y __ __ __ __

4. __ __ __ D __ __ F __ __

5. __ __ S C __ __ A __ __ __

6. __ __ T __ __ F __ __ __

7. V __ __ __ __ __ U __ __

8. __ __ __ __ Y __ __ __ __

9. V __ __ __ __ __ __ Y

10. __ __ __ __ I __ __ D

11. __ __ __ __ __ F __ I

12. __ F F __ __ __ __ __ __ __

13. __ __ U __ __ R __

14. __ __ C E __ __ __

15. C __ __ __ __ __ __ E __

Vivacious	Affectionate	Fascinated
Delighted	Satisfied	Loving
Joyous	Wonderful	Vitality
Pleasant	Peaceful	Rapture
Infatuated	Enjoying	Ecstatic

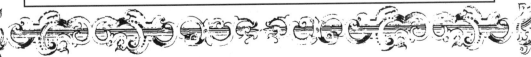

Name _____ Date _____

AFFECTION

Directions: How would you express your feelings of affection in each of the following situations? Write the information on the lines.

	What do you say?	*What do you do?*
1. Your friend got an A on his history paper	_____	_____
2. Your mother had a new baby	_____	_____
3. The track team has won the championship	_____	_____
4. The new boy/girl said he/she likes you	_____	_____
5. Your friend has finished a drug treatment program	_____	_____
6. Your sister's poster has won first prize	_____	_____
7. The teacher of the year is your teacher	_____	_____
8. Your older brother was chosen in the football draft	_____	_____

Starter Words:

Smile   I Like You   Handshake   Grin   Pat on the Back

SOCIAL SKILL
Understanding Fear

Behavioral Objective: Students will understand that fear is a universal experience that may alert you to danger.

Directed Lesson:

1. ***Establish the Need:*** Students need to realize that fear, like pain, is a feeling of recognition of a negative situation that needs to be dealt with, and becomes a "negative" feeling in our perception when an appropriate effective behavior is not immediately available. They need to learn how to search for, choose, and utilize behaviors to cope realistically with the situation.

2. ***Introduction:*** Share the following vignettes, suggesting to the class that some of the fears they will hear about are realistic, while others are not:

   "Joe very cautiously steps into his room. Careful not to close the door, he looks around, under, and behind every piece of furniture in the room, checking for the poisonous snake that might be hiding somewhere. Only then does he close the door, cutting off his escape route."

   "A group of people enters the elevator in the high-rise building. About halfway to the top floor, the elevator stops with a loud grinding noise. A few seconds later, it suddenly drops about a foot. It is stuck between floors. The lights flicker and dim."

   "You are riding in a car with a friend. After you got into the car, your friend told you that the car was 'borrowed.' You realize that means it was stolen. Just then you hear a siren, and you look back to see the lights flashing on the police car behind you."

3. ***Identify the Skill Components:*** List the following skill components on the board or on sentence strips.

   1. Decide if you are feeling afraid.
   2. Admit to yourself that you *are* afraid.
   3. Think about and identify what may be causing the fear.
   4. Determine if there is more than one cause for fear; if so, how many, and what kind?
   5. Decide whether the fear is realistic (would it be foolish *not* to be afraid?).
   6. Figure out the worst thing that can happen.
   7. Figure out the best outcome you can hope for.
   8. Choose the behavior most likely to remove, change, or lessen the situation causing the fear.

4.　**Model the Skill:** The teacher and student will role play the following scenario: A boy was playing baseball with a friend. Suddenly, the ball accidentally went through a neighbor's window. This neighbor had often complained to the police about kids tramping through his yard and playing ball in front of his house. This time, he has yelled from the house that he's going to sue someone's parents for his window.

　　A. What action can the student take to alleviate his fear?

　　B. How can he stop his parents from being sued?

5.　**Behavioral Rehearsal:**

　　A. *Selection:* Divide the class into groups of four. Assign each group one of the vignettes already used. Students not required to role play should participate as spectators who can advise the principal role players.

　　B. *Role Play:* In sequence, groups identify their situation, then role play. For the first vignette one student can be a friend who enters the room with Joe. For this and the other roll plays the "spectators" can be active (give advice as the scene is played), or passive (respond with suggestions following role play).

　　C. *Completion:* After each role play, reinforce correct behavior, identify inappropriate behavior, and reenact the role play with corrections. If there are no corrections, role play is complete.

　　D　*Reinforcers:* Give verbal and nonverbal praise (specific) for correct behavior.

　　E. *Discussion:* Discuss the role play and have students talk about the fear. Stimulate discussion by asking a few questions. Here are some examples:

　　　　– What fears help us to protect ourselves from dangerous situations?

　　　　　　Fear of being hit by a car.

　　　　　　Fear of going to jail for committing a crime.

　　　　　　Fear of violent situations, fear of being hurt.

　　　　– What kind of fear is unrealistic?

　　　　　　Fear of being poisoned by eating a candy.

　　　　　　Fear of being hit by an airplane.

　　　　　　Fear of things coming alive.

　　　　　　Fear of crossing the street against the light.

6.　**Practice:** Distribute copies of the worksheet "Fear Word Puzzle" for students to complete. Answers are below.

DOWN		ACROSS	
1.	intimidate	3.	concern
2.	panic	4.	scared
4.	startled	5.	anxious
6.	helpless	7.	frightened
8.	fearful	11.	terrified
9.	uneasy	12.	spiteful
10.	nervous		

> *Note:* Point out to students that one word (12) is not exactly a "fear" word, but names a feeling that may be directed toward a person or situation as a result of fear.

7. **Independent Use:** Distribute copies of the worksheet "Now What?" Call attention to Skill Components #6 and #7, and point out that they form the "boundaries" of problems posed by the fear-inducing situation, and that Skill Component #8 is the "tool" or "weapon" to be used to "make the fear go away" by effectively dealing with it. Insure that the students recognize that the sheet to be taken home follows these Skill Components in sequence as a problem-solving device.

8. **Continuation:** Teacher should continue pointing out the need for this skill as related situations arise.

Name _____ Date _____

FEAR WORD PUZZLE

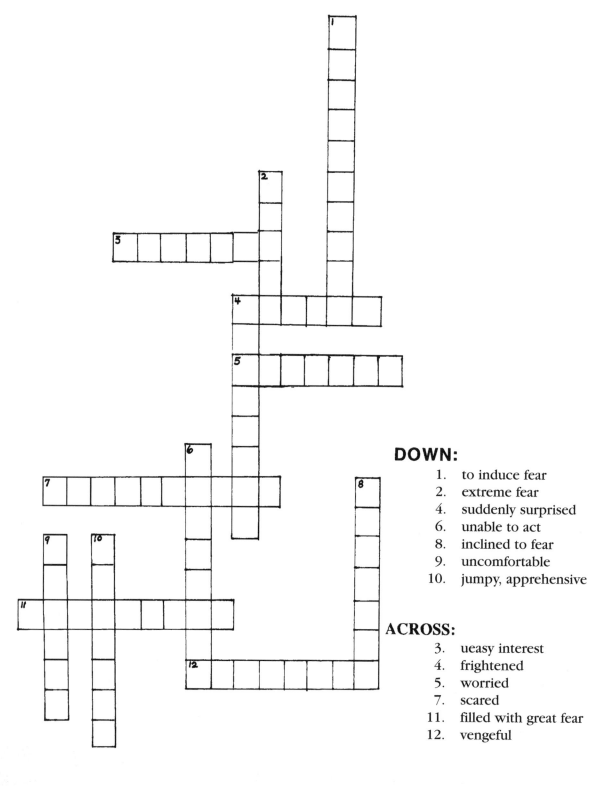

DOWN:

1. to induce fear
2. extreme fear
4. suddenly surprised
6. unable to act
8. inclined to fear
9. uncomfortable
10. jumpy, apprehensive

ACROSS:

3. ueasy interest
4. frightened
5. worried
7. scared
11. filled with great fear
12. vengeful

Name _____ Date _____

NOW WHAT?

DIRECTIONS: You are faced with the following situations. Decide the following for each:

> **A.** What is the **worst** that can happen?
> **B.** What is the **best** you can hope for?
> **C.** What would you **choose** to do?

1. Earlier this morning at home you were swinging a stick by the TV set and you "broke" the screen.

A.   (Worst)   _____
B.   (Best)   _____
C.   (Choose) _____

2. Your science teacher just told you that you are getting an "F" on your report card. You've been telling your parents that you are doing well in science.

A.   (Worst)   _____
B.   (Best)   _____
C.   (Choose) _____

3. Your mother has given you money to buy food at the store. Along the way you lose the money.

A.   (Worst)   _____
B.   (Best)   _____
C.   (Choose) _____

4. The principal has called you to the office.

A.   (Worst)   _____
B.   (Best)   _____
C.   (Choose) _____

5. Someone in school told a student with a reputation for being a "fighter that YOU want to fight. Now you've heard that this student is looking for you.
A.   (Worst)   _____
B.   (Best)   _____
C.   (Choose) _____

6. Your friend loaned you a tape player and you dropped it and it broke.
A.   (Worst)   _____
B.   (Best)   _____
C.   (Choose) _____

SOCIAL SKILL

Managing the Emotion (Fear)

Behavioral Objective: Students will understand that fear is a normal and universal experience that can be identified and overcome.

Directed Lesson:

1. **Establish the Need:** Students need to realize that fear is a necessary emotion. It is positive when it leads to recognition of a threat. It is negative if no remedy can be found. Learning to manage your fear is an essential skill.

2. **Introduction:** Share the following vignettes, suggesting to the class the need to discriminate between realistic and unrealistic fears:

    (a) "Roxanne's best friend was killed in an automobile accident only three weeks ago. Today she accepted a ride to school with a neighbor who has been driving over 35 years and never had an accident or received a ticket. On the way to school Roxanne suddenly looked up and saw a car speeding directly toward them, just as she heard the driver shout, 'We're going to crash!'"

    (b) "You and a friend are visiting someone you know who lives on the fourth floor of an apartment building. Your host invites you both to look out the window at a group of people running around on the other side of the street below. Your friend takes a quick look, gasps, and jumps back. When asked 'What's wrong?' your friend says, 'I'm afraid I'll fall.'"

    (c) "Dan has had his new skateboard long enough to do better with it than any of his friends. He has boasted that he can do more and better tricks than anybody. He says his friends are afraid to do anything that could hurt themselves. His friends dare him to ride his skateboard back and forth across a busy highway near his home. He accepts."

3. **Identify the Skill Components:** Write the following skill components on the board or on sentence strips.

    1. Decide if you are feeling afraid.
    2. Admit your fear to yourself.
    3. Identify what is causing the fear.
    4. Speculate as to whether there is more than one cause for this fear.
    5. Decide whether the fear is realistic.
    6. Think about the worst that can happen.

    7. Explore the best you can hope for.

    8. Decide what is in your power to change.

    9. Choose behavior most likely to remove, change, or lessen your fear.

4.   ***Model the Skill:*** The teacher will role play a situation where he/she had experienced a fear and will demonstrate how using the skill component steps helped to overcome the fear.

5.   ***Behavioral Rehearsal:***

    A. *Selection:* Teacher selects groups of three students to role play each vignette.

    B. *Role Play:* The students may use the three vignettes given in the Introduction to role play. They may also design and use their own scenario if they wish.

    C. *Completion:* After each role play, reinforce correct behavior, identify inappropriate behaviors, and reenact role play with corrections. If there are no corrections, role play is complete.

    D. *Reinforcers:* Give verbal and nonverbal praise (specific).

    E. *Discussion:* Students will discuss the importance of the emotion fear. Using the skill components they will tell how to correctly respond to situations involving fear. Students will discuss examples of positive and negative fears. They will discuss ways to use fear to their advantage.

6.   ***Practice:*** Distribute copies of the following worksheet, "Fear Scrambles Me." Collect when finished.

7.   ***Independent Use:*** Have students take home the worksheet entitled "Fears." Ask them to answer the questions and then write a short story about a fear situation.

8.   ***Continuation:*** Teacher should continue to point out the need for this skill as related situations arise.

Name _____   Date _____

FEAR SCRAMBLES ME

Directions: Unscramble the words below and write them on the line. Use the **FEAR WORDS** at the bottom to help you.

1. tteaminidi   _____

2. nacip   _____

3. delsatrt   _____

4. pellhess   _____

5. htegrifden   _____

6. nasyue   _____

7. servnuo   _____

8. dietreifr   _____

9. fitesplu   _____

10. nrecnoc   _____

11. darecs   _____

12. axsnuoi   _____

FEAR WORDS		
terrified	spiteful	intimidate
helpless	panic	scared
concern	nervous	uneasy
startled	anxious	frightened

Name _____ Date _____

F E A R S

Directions: Here are some "fear" situations. Decide how you would react and fill in the blank. Then, compare your reasons with those of your classmates. Can you learn another way to react?

1. When I am frightened, I _____

2. I feel helpless when _____

3. When I feel panic, I _____

4. _____ makes me nervous.

5. I sometimes like to intimidate _____

6. I was startled when _____

7. Once I felt terrified and I _____

8. I feel concern for others when _____

9. When I'm feeling anxious, I _____

10. I feel spiteful when _____

11. I feel uneasy when I am around _____

12. When _____ happens, I feel fearful!

BECOME A PROBLEM SOLVER. On the back of this page, write a story about a fearful person who seeks help in an effort to overcome fears. Outline your story below.

SOCIAL SKILL
Rewarding Yourself

Behavioral Objective: Students will learn that rewarding themselves is a way to motivate themselves.

Directed Lesson:

1. ***Establish the Need:*** Major goals in one's life sometimes seem unattainable. By setting minor goals and rewarding oneself when those minor goals are reached, the major goals will not seem so far away. Rewarding yourself is an excellent way to foster self-motivation.

2. ***Introduction:*** Tell the following story:

    "**Rod was on the track team for his school. He had tried out for a number of events—the pole vault, the broad jump, and the high hurdles. He was good enough to be happy about his performance in all of them, but the coach tried him out in several other events and told Rod he wanted him to concentrate on the 440 meters. Coach said Rod was the best he had seen in that distance in a number of years. He told Rod, 'If you work hard enough, you have what it takes to break the all-time school record in the 440.'**

    "**Rod practiced every day even to the point of making the 440 run in a park near his home for additional practice. He beat every other member of the team by 10 to 15 steps in competition. But that school record bugged him. He thought about it. In his dreams he could hear the roar of the crowd when he finally broke the record. What a feeling!**

    "**One day Rod went to the high school track late in the afternoon. He was all alone. He had his stop watch with him. He drew in a deep breath, and let it out slowly. Something told him, This is the day! He set himself, heard the starting gun go off in his brain, pressed the button on the stop watch, and burst into action. At the finish, he pressed the button again. Did he dare look at the time? Finally he did. He beat the school record by 7 seconds! 7 seconds! And no one to see it—no crowd to cheer—no medal or trophy to take home.**"

3. ***Identify the Skill Components:*** List the skill components on the board or sentence strips:

    1. Decide which goals will be rewarded.
    2. Determine the rewards.
    3. Set out to achieve your goal.
    4. Reward yourself when the goal is achieved.

4. ***Model the Skill:*** Teacher chooses an accomplishment requiring enough skill to be at least mildly difficult, then demonstrates practice of the skill with some degree of failure before success is achieved on the third or fourth attempt. Examples:

   ▶ touching toes

   ▶ saying a tongue-twister (e.g., "The two-twenty-two train to Tooting tooted tunefully as it tore through the tunnel" or "She sells sea shells by the sea shore")

   ▶ quoting something from memory (e.g., list of states or state capitals, a short poem, a short list of historical facts)

   Teacher then tells the class how he or she would reward him/herself for accomplishing the modeled task.

5. ***Behavioral Rehearsal:***

   A. *Selection:* Teacher divides students into groups of three.

   B. *Role Play:* Remind students of the story of Rod's achievement told in the Introduction. Suggest a few other kinds of achievements, such as:

      – learning to ride a unicycle

      – completing a walk-a-thon

      – passing a test when the student is expected to fail

      – getting a job

      – winning a prize

      Each student in the group is to tell the others what achievement he/she is role playing and what he/she has chosen to say or do for a self-reward. Teacher chooses one of the groups to report to the class and to reenact the role play.

   C. *Completion:* After each role play, reinforce the correct behavior, identify inappropriate behaviors, and reenact the role play with corrections. If there are no corrections, the role play is complete.

   D. *Reinforcers:* Acknowledge appropriate behaviors with verbal and nonverbal praise (specific).

   E. *Discussion:* Provide the students opportunities to evaluate the role play, indicating appropriate and inappropriate behaviors. Further, they may discuss their personal accomplishments and rewards.

6. ***Practice:*** Distribute the worksheet "Interview" to students. Suggest that the best responses would be either (1) something they have actually done, or (2) something they genuinely aspire to do.

7. ***Independent Use:*** Hand out the worksheet "I Can" for students to take home to be shared with the family. (Perhaps parents can and will allow themselves to be involved in suggesting and enabling the reward factor in C.) Students are asked to bring the completed worksheet back to class to share it with teacher and peers.

8. ***Continuation:*** Teachers should continue pointing out the need for this skill as related situations arise.

Name _____ Date _____

INTERVIEW

Directions: You entered a newspaper contest entitled **"I DESERVE A REWARD BECAUSE"** and wrote an essay. Today you are being interviewed by a reporter. Who in the class will win the award? Take a vote.

REPORTER: What have you done to deserve an award?

YOU:_____

_____

REPORTER: Is there a way to verbally reward yourself?

YOU:_____

_____

REPORTER: How could you actively reward yourself?

YOU:_____

_____

EXAMPLES: Here are some suggestions to get you started, but you are to make up your own idea for something that is worthy of an award.

You saved a young child from a speeding car.

You helped a neighbor with yard work all year.

You called for help when a fire was starting.

Name _____   Date _____

I CAN

"You need not be perfect nor do everything perfectly in order to find good things about yourself that can be rewarded."

Directions: List some positive statements about yourself in response to each of the following questions.

A. What can I do now?

   1. _____
   2. _____
   3. _____
   4. _____
   5. _____

B. What can I do when I put my mind to it?

   1. _____
   2. _____
   3. _____
   4. _____
   5. _____

C. When I prove to myself what I can do, how will I reward myself?

   1. _____
   2. _____
   3. _____
   4. _____
   5. _____

SOCIAL SKILL
Rewarding Yourself for Achievement

Behavioral Objective: Students will use self-rewards when they have obtained a personal goal.

Directed Lesson:

1. ***Establish the Need:*** Students are constantly reminded by adults of the need to be successful in all aspects of life. In order to meet large goals, many times smaller goals have to be met first. Students need to be motivated to meet both the small goals as well as the large goals. Self-rewarding is one way in which students may be able to keep themselves motivated.

2. ***Introduction:*** Ask and solicit answers for the following:

    ❱ What change would you like to make in your appearance? How will you reward yourself after you make that change?

    ❱ What personality traits would you like to acquire? After you acquire this trait, how will your life be different?

    ❱ What future goal will you be working for to feel successful? Your reward for achieving this will be _____.

3. ***Identify the Skill Components:*** Write the skill components on the board or on sentence strips.

    1. Develop an attitude of "self-reward."
    2. Decide what accomplishments should be rewarded.
    3. Relate rewards to accomplishment.
    4. Accept "self-rewards" to motivate success.
    5. Admit success feels good.
    6. Reward yourself.

4. ***Model the Skill:*** The teacher relates an example of personal accomplishment and self-reward. The skill components will be used to illustrate the steps in this process.

5. ***Behavioral Rehearsal:***

    A. *Selection:* Teacher divides students into groups of three.
    B. *Role Plays:*

        –   Interviewing for a job and getting it
        –   Being part of an athletic team

 - Improving one or more grades
 - Making honor role or merit role
 - Making citizenship role, or perfect attendance
 - Achieving weight loss or gain
 - Making more friends

Each member of the group is to tell the others what achievement he/she has chosen, what the sub-goals are, and the chosen verbal and/or material self-rewards. The group chooses one of these to report back to the class and reenact the situations.

C. *Completion:* After each role play, reinforce the correct behavior, identify incorrect behaviors, and reenact with corrections. If there are no corrections, the role play is complete.

D. *Reinforcers:* Reinforce correct behavior with verbal and nonverbal praise (specific).

E. *Discussion:* The students' level of performance is evaluated by peers and inappropriate behaviors are corrected. Elicit the students' opinions of giving themselves rewards.

6. ***Practice:*** Distribute copies of the worksheet "What's Your Goal?" for students to complete in class. Then call on volunteers to share some of their goals and discuss these with the class.

7. ***Independent Use:*** Send home the worksheet "What's the Payoff?" Encourage students to choose additional short and intermediate goals and appropriate rewards.

8. ***Continuation:*** Teacher should continue pointing out the need for this skill as related situations arise.

Name _____ Date _____

WHAT'S YOUR GOAL?

Directions: Compare your present behavior and actions with the way you would like to be. Then set for yourself some short-term and long-term goals for the time periods given below.

Example: I don't go to bed early therefore I get sleepy in class.
GOAL: I will go to bed at _____P.M.

WEEKLY GOAL 1 _____

_____

WEEKLY GOAL 2 _____

_____

MONTHLY GOAL 1 _____

_____

MONTHLY GOAL 2 _____

_____

6-MONTH GOAL 1 _____

_____

6-MONTH GOAL 2 _____

_____

YEARLY GOAL 1 _____

_____

YEARLY GOAL 2 _____

_____

Name _____ Date _____

WHAT'S THE PAYOFF?

Directions: When you reach a goal that you have set, you feel great! Sometimes that feeling is a reward in itself. At other times, people like to "give themselves a reward." How could you reward yourself for the goals that you have <u>set</u> and <u>met</u>? Record your answers below.

FOR REACHING MY DAILY GOAL, I WILL

1. _____

2. _____

FOR REACHING MY WEEKLY GOAL, I WILL

1. _____

2. _____

FOR REACHING MY MONTHLY GOAL, I WILL

1. _____

2. _____

FOR REACHING MY YEARLY GOAL, I WILL

1. _____

2. _____

SOCIAL SKILL

Responding to a Need for Help

Behavioral Objective: The student will recognize an individual in need of help and decide upon an appropriate method of assistance.

Directed Lesson:

1. ***Establish the Need:*** Helping another person is an admirable and rewarding experience. This skill will be useful in all aspects of your life (i.e., school, home, community, and work).

2. ***Introduction:*** Read the following story:

   "John and Sue were at home watching television one night. In the middle of the show, they heard a young girl screaming for help. They ran to the window, looked out, and saw a girl being chased by a man. She was yelling, 'Help me, help me.' John and Sue were not sure what action to take and discussed what they could possibly do to help the girl. They finally decided to call the police.

   "When the police car appeared, a crowd gathered on the street. On the sidewalk was the body of a young girl who appeared to be 13 or 14 years of age."

   The teacher asks the class three questions: (1) **"Why do you think no one responded immediately to the girl's screams?"** (2) **"If someone had responded immediately, could the ending of the story been different?"** (3) **"How so?"**

3. ***Identify the Skill Components:*** List the following skill components on the board.

   1. Recognize when a person really needs help.
   2. Ask the person if he/she needs assistance.
   3. Ask the person what kind of help is needed.
   4. Choose a correct response to the situation.
   5. Follow through with appropriate assistance.
   6. In case of danger, stay in a safe place and call the police—911.

4. ***Model the Skill:*** The teacher will show the class how he/she would follow the skill components if he/she saw someone in need of help.

5. ***Behavioral Rehearsal:***

   A. *Selection:* The entire class discusses the modeled skill. The teacher selects groups of three students to role play.

    B. *Role Play:* Two groups of students will demonstrate appropriate helping behavior and two groups will demonstrate non-helping behavior.

    C. *Completion:* If there are no corrections, the role play is complete. If there are corrections, state the corrections and model the appropriate helping behaviors.

    D. *Reinforcers:* Teacher and classmates should use verbal praise to acknowledge correct behavior.

    E. *Discussion:* Discuss ways that students can be helpful at home, at school, and in their community.

6. ***Practice:*** Distribute copies of the worksheet "Helping Others" to the class and ask students to answer the questions in complete sentences.

    1. **In the past week, how have you helped a family member?**

    2. **In the past week, how have you helped a classmate?**

    3. **In the past week, how and when have you helped a stranger?**

7. ***Independent Use:*** Give students copies of the worksheet entitled "Photo Highlights: Helping Others" to take home. They are to look for examples of people helping one another from TV, radio, newspapers, magazines, and personal observations, and complete the worksheet. Students will receive verbal rewards for sharing their findings with the class.

8. ***Continuation:*** Teacher tells students, "If you use this skill whenever and wherever you need it, others will feel good about you and you will feel good about yourself."

Name _____ Date _____

HELPING OTHERS

Directions: Answer each of the following questions, using complete sentences.

1. In the past week, how have you helped a family member?

2. In the past week, how have you helped a classmate?

3. In the past week, how and when did you help a stranger?

4. How did helping someone else make you feel?

Name _____ Date _____

PHOTO HIGHLIGHTS: HELPING OTHERS

Directions: Use a variety of newspapers and magazines to look for pictures that show examples of people helping one another. Cut them out, arrange, and paste them below.

SOCIAL SKILL
Feeling Good About Helping

Behavioral Objective: Students will feel self-satisfaction upon giving assistance to others.

Directed Lesson:

1. **Establish the Need:** Giving assistance to someone else is an admirable and rewarding experience. This skill may give you self-satisfaction, open the door for unexpected opportunities (e.g., experience, job promotions, job opportunities), or motivate others to help you when *you* need assistance.

2. **Introduction:** The teacher will read the following story to the class:

   "**Early one morning, Richard and a group of his friends were on their way to school. Several blocks from their neighborhood, they saw an elderly woman lying on the sidewalk. They all kept walking to school, but Richard decided to turn around and walk back to the woman. He knelt down beside her. She could barely speak, but Richard was able to understand her. She asked him to get her some help. Richard went to a house nearby and asked the inhabitants to dial 911 for the lady. An emergency vehicle came and took her to a hospital.**

   "**While the lady was recovering in the hospital from a broken hip, she received Richard's name and address from the police. She sent Richard a beautiful thank-you card with a five-dollar bill tucked inside. Richard was surprised. He and his parents decided to visit the lady in the hospital, and a friendship was formed.**

   "**Richard began doing odd jobs for the lady. He continued working for her until he graduated from high school. Many years later, the woman died and Richard was informed by the lady's lawyer that his name was included in her will.**"

   Ask students to respond to these questions: Why did Richard turn around and go back to help the woman? Would you have stopped to offer help? Why or why not?

3. **Identify Skill Components:** List the following skill components on the board or on sentence strips:

   1. Recognize that a person needs help.
   2. Ask the person if he/she needs assistance.
   3. Ask the person what kind of assistance he/she needs.
   4. Choose a correct response to the situation.
   5. Remain in a safe place in case of danger, and dial 911.
   6. Follow through with an appropriate response to the situation.

7. Notice how you feel after you have helped someone.

8. Notice whether more people are inclined to help you after you have helped someone.

4. ***Model the Skill:*** The teacher will pretend to receive a telephone call from the American Cancer Society. The society asks the teacher to do the fundraising collection on her street. The teacher agrees.

5. ***Behavioral Rehearsal:***

   A. *Selection:* One student at a time.

   B. *Role Play:* Students will role play the telephone call from the American Cancer Society and the story in the introduction. They will give their response to both situations.

   C. *Completion:* Students will comment on the role play. If no corrections are needed, the role play is complete.

   D. *Reinforcers:* Correct behavior should be acknowledged by positive comments from teacher and peers.

   E. *Discussion:* Teacher should discuss the idea that you should help others because you want to or because it makes you feel good, not because you *will* get something out of it. Sometimes helping one person will benefit many people and maybe yourself indirectly.

6. ***Practice:*** Have students complete the following worksheet "Mail-a-Gram" which is a mail-a-gram written by a community leader asking the students for help on a clean-up project.

7. ***Independent Use:*** Give students copies of the worksheet entitled "The 'Lend A Hand' Group" for completion in class or as a take-home assignment. Students can complete part or all of the worksheet telling how they helped others.

8. ***Continuation:*** Teacher will continue to point out the need for this skill in all situations. They also might make new friends by using this skill.

Name _____

Date _____

MAIL-A-GRAM

Dear Students:

On Saturday from 9:00 A.M. to 3:00 P.M., we will have a clean-up in our community. We need your help in keeping our community neat, clean, and attractive. Complete this study sheet and return it to your teacher. Write a paragraph below about what YOU can do to help, and your reasons for participating in this project.

_____

_____

_____

_____

_____

_____

_____

Name _____ Date _____

JOIN THE "LEND A HAND" GROUP

Directions: Prepare a list of all of the people you have helped recently. Describe how you helped each person, how it made you feel, and whether your helping them has made a difference in your own life. (Use the back of this page if you need more space.)

1.

2.

3.

4.

5.

911   HELP!   FEEL GOOD

SOCIAL SKILL

Using Negotiation to Settle Difficulties

Behavioral Objective: Students will use negotiation as an alternative to aggression when involved in a confrontation with others.

Directed Lesson:

1. **Establish the Need:** Use of this skill will allow people to live more harmonious lives. Teachers should stress that incidents of violence will decrease when people learn to settle their differences by negotiation.

2. **Introduction:**

    "Have you ever done something you knew was wrong, but you did it anyway because your friends (known as peers) encouraged you to and you wanted to keep their friendship? This is called *negative peer pressure*. Peer pressure can also be positive when it results in appropriate behavior. If you decide not to participate with a group that exerts negative peer pressure, you can attempt to negotiate and reach a compromise that permits you to do the right things without risking your friendship with the group. If this doesn't work, it will be to your best interest to make new friends whose attitude and behavior is more like yours."

3. **Identify the Skill Components:** List the following skill components on the board or on sentence strips.

    1. Decide if there is a problem between you and any other person(s).
    2. Inform that person or those persons about what you think is the problem.
    3. Meet face to face to discuss the problem.
    4. Listen to each other with open minds.
    5. Respect each other's opinions.
    6. Take a few minutes to recycle the other person's opinions in your mind.
    7. Try to determine why he/she felt that way.
    8. Avoid "finger-pointing."
    9. Try to work out a compromise that pleases both of you.

4. **Model the Skill:** Two students will have a "mock" argument in which one student is trying to convince the other to do something in order to belong to the group since they know it would not be appropriate behavior (e.g, cut school and go downtown). These students will then sit down and go through the steps of negotiation to solve their problem.

5. ***Behavioral Rehearsal:*** The students are given an opportunity to perform the behavior and be evaluated.

    A. *Selection:* Teacher will have pairs of volunteers come to the front of the classroom.

    B. *Role Play:* Each pair of students will be told or given a situation on cards to negotiate with each other. They will go through the skill steps of negotiation to reach a compromise and give example situations.

    C. *Completion:* After each role play, the class will reinforce correct behavior, identify inappropriate behaviors, and a new group of volunteers will reenact the role play with corrections.

    D. *Reinforcers:* Have the class verbally praise those students who went through the negotiation process correctly.

    E. *Discussion:* Teacher leads a discussion on ways in which negotiation techniques can be used to avoid gang violence, and problems between friends, family, and school.

6. ***Practice:*** Hand out copies of the worksheet "Sharpen Your Negotiating Skills" and ask the class to complete the worksheet by using the words listed at the top of the page. After they have completed the worksheet, students will exchange and correct each other's papers.

7. ***Independent Use:*** Give students copies of the following story starter entitled "The Pencil Problem" and ask them to finish the story by using negotiating skill steps to resolve the problem.

8. ***Continuation:*** Teacher should continue pointing out the need for this skill as related situations arise.

Name _____ Date _____

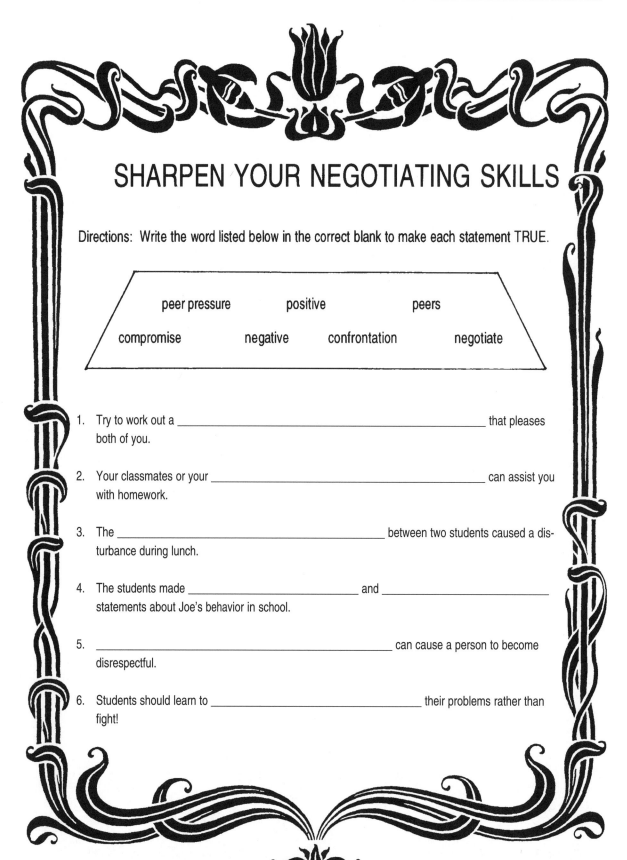

SHARPEN YOUR NEGOTIATING SKILLS

Directions: Write the word listed below in the correct blank to make each statement TRUE.

> peer pressure   positive   peers
>
> compromise   negative   confrontation   negotiate

1. Try to work out a _____ that pleases both of you.

2. Your classmates or your _____ can assist you with homework.

3. The _____ between two students caused a disturbance during lunch.

4. The students made _____ and _____ statements about Joe's behavior in school.

5. _____ can cause a person to become disrespectful.

6. Students should learn to _____ their problems rather than fight!

Name _____ Date _____

THE PENCIL PROBLEM

Directions: Write a story using the story starter written below. In the story, include some of the negotiating steps to resolve the problem.

Jose and Juan were arguing over a new blue pencil. Jose had picked it up from the floor when he came into the room. That's when Juan grabbed it and shoved it into his pocket..........

SOCIAL SKILL

Using Negotiation to Deal with Peer Pressure

Behavioral Objective: Students will use negotiation as a technique for dealing with peer pressure as it relates to inappropriate behaviors such as drugs, teen sex, and gang activity.

Directed Lesson:

1. ***Establish the Need:*** The teacher should stress to the students that incidents of violence will decrease when people learn to settle their differences by negotiating. Negotiation will also allow students to learn to make their own choices and accept the consequences of their choice.

2. ***Introduction:*** Teacher will lead a class discussion on the following:

    ◗ Suppose you go to a party and realize that it's not the place where you want to be?
      - Who do you tell?
      - How do you leave?

    ◗ Suppose your friends try to pressure you into staying?
      - Think of at least three ways to make a graceful exit.

3. ***Identify the Skill Components:*** Write the following skill components on the board or on sentence strips.

    1. Identify the problem.
    2. Formulate your opinion.
    3. Discuss it with peer(s).
    4. Listen to each other with open minds.
    5. Respect each other's opinions.
    6. Avoid "finger-pointing."
    7. Work out a compromise that pleases both of you.
    8. Make your choice of what to do.
    9. Live and abide by your choice.
    10. Ask "Do I feel good about my decision?"

4. ***Model the Skill:*** The teacher will model the following situation as if she/he were a tenth grader:

    The teacher/student goes to a party and realizes that he/she does not belong with this group. He/she models ways to leave the party:

> ❱ Phone a friend or family member and ask to be picked up.

> ❱ Tell your best friend, and decide to leave together.

> ❱ Just walk out the door, and go home.

5. ***Behavioral Rehearsal:***

   A. *Selection:* Select one boy and one girl at a time.

   B. *Role Play:* Each group will role play the situation presented by the teacher when modeling the skills, remembering to use the skill components.

   C. *Completion:* After each role play, the class will reinforce correct behavior, identify inappropriate behaviors, and a new group of volunteers will reenact the role play with corrections.

   D. *Reinforcers:* Have the class applaud for each group of actors.

   E. *Discussion:* Teacher will ask students to talk about the following:

      – What would you do if you were the person invited to the party? (Get prior information.)

      – What would you do if your best friend decided to stay, but you felt uneasy?

      – Would you be proud of yourself if someone you cared for (mother, father, grandmother, teacher, etc.) learned that you were at this party?

      – What does this mean: "We are judged by the company we keep"?

6. ***Practice:*** Hand out copies of the following worksheet, "It's *Your* Choice." Ask students to complete the worksheet and return it to you for a class discussion.

7. ***Independent Use:*** Distribute copies of the worksheet entitled "A Family Curfew Compromise" to the class. Students will conduct a family interview and negotiate with parents how to get permission to come home at a later hour. Write down how the negotiations went and what the compromise was.

8. ***Continuation:*** Teacher should continue pointing out the importance of making your own choices before acting and not giving in to peer pressure.

Name _____ Date _____

IT'S *YOUR* CHOICE

Directions: Working with a classmate, choose one of the following statements and write a paragraph explaining why you agree or disagree with the statement. You and your partner must be in total agreement. HELPFUL HINT: Remember to negotiate and compromise with each other.

* *

CHOOSE YOUR STATEMENT:

1. **Drugs should be legalized.**
2. **The welfare system does not really help people improve their living standard.**
3. **Students should not be required by law to attend school.**
4. **It's OK to exercise peer pressure to have people do "things" in order to be part of the group.**

Name _____ Date _____

A FAMILY CURFEW COMPROMISE

Directions: Discuss the following situation with each member of your family and write down their responses in the space provided below.

Your friends say that they can stay out as long as they wish on a school night. Your parents insist that you be home before it gets dark. You know the other kids will tease you if they know that you have a curfew. Using negotiation skills, can you and your parents work out a compromise?

_____

_____

_____

_____

_____

_____

_____

_____

_____

_____

_____

_____

_____

_____

SOCIAL SKILL
Staying Calm Under Stress

Behavioral Objective: The students will learn to use new strategies for remaining calm under stress.

Directed Lesson:

1. **Establish the Need:** Throughout a person's lifetime, he/she will be faced with many stressful situations. It is important that a person uses "self-control" to stay "cool" when dealing with such situations.

2. **Introduction:** Point out to the class that "stress" can be "harmful" as well as "helpful" to an individual. Give examples of situations that can cause stress such as: moving to a new neighborhood, transferring to a new school, having a divorce in the family, suffering with a headache or an ulcer. An example of helpful stress is being frightened by a noise at the door. The noise alerts you and causes you to be on guard. By using self-control an individual can decrease stress. Serious problems can be solved only when using self-control. Emphasize the point that self-control is vital for "survival" in today's world.

3. **Identify the Skill Components:** Write the following skill components on the board or on sentence strips.

   1. Recognize the problem that's causing you to lose your self-control.
   2. Identify your feelings (anger, fear).
   3. Decide what happened to make you feel this way.
   4. Discuss the situation.
   5. Focus on positive outcomes.
   6. Strive for self-control (count to ten), stay "cool."
   7. Accept situations you cannot change.
   8. Inform the teacher or some adult about the problem.
   9. Choose the skills you need to control yourself and to feel comfortable.

4. **Model the Skill:** Two students will be playfully teasing each other. One of the two students becomes upset and wants to start fighting. The class will discuss how the student who wants to fight can control his/her emotions without a fight.

   The teacher will direct the discussion by constantly emphasizing how the skill components can be used successfully in controlling the situation.

5. **Behavioral Rehearsal:**

    A. *Selection:* Two pairs of students are selected to role play a situation involving self-control.

    B. *Role Play:* Students will act out the following situation:

        A student accidentally bumps into another student in the hall, and the student drops his/her books:

        –   Student apologizes and helps pick up the books

        –   Student identifies feelings (annoyance)

        –   Annoyed student exhibits self-control by counting to ten

        Have students make a list of healthy stress situations such as being alarmed by the sound of the fire bell, or a tornado warning drill.

    C. *Completion:* After each role play, the teacher and class will reinforce the correct behavior and identify inappropriate behaviors that they observed during the role play.

    D. *Reinforcers:* The students and teacher will applaud the role players every time the role players use the appropriate behavior during their presentation.

    E. *Discussion:* Discuss the role playing and have the students identify the skill components they recognized during the role playing activity.

6. **Practice:** Distribute copies of the following "Personal Record Sheet" to the class. Students are to use this to record any incident at home in which they were involved and were successful in using one or more of the skill components to maintain self-control.

7. **Independent Use:** Give students copies of the worksheet entitled "Featuring: An Example of Self-Control." They are to write a paragraph about a television show or movie that involved the use of self-control and return the write-up to the teacher at the end of the week. They will describe the incident and write about the skill components that were used to solve the conflict.

8. **Continuation:** The teacher should continue to stress the need for this skill as related situations arise.

Name _____ Date _____

PERSONAL RECORD SHEET

Directions: Place a check each day in the appropriate column every time you use one of the self-control skill components at home. Also, write a brief phrase about each incident in the space provided <u>below</u> the chart. EXAMPLE: "It's not my turn to wash the dishes."

SKILL COMPONENTS	M	T	W	T	F
Choose the skill components you need for control.					
Inform someone about the problem.					
Leave, or walk away.					
Accept situations that you cannot change.					
Focus on positive outcomes.					
Control your emotions— count to ten.					
Negotiate the stressful situation, if possible.					
Identify your feelings.					
Recognize the problem.					

_____

_____

_____

_____

Name _____   Date _____

FEATURING: AN EXAMPLE OF SELF-CONTROL

Directions: Write a paragraph about a TV show or movie that involved the use of self-control. Describe the incident and identify the skill components used to promote self-control. Return this worksheet to your teacher at the end of the week.

SOCIAL SKILL
Recognizing Loss of Self-Control

Behavioral Objective: The students will learn and use strategies for recognizing the internal changes in the body that signal they are about to lose self-control.

Directed Lesson:

1. **Establish the Need:** During a person's life expectancy, he/she will need to know and recognize that internal forces, as well as external forces, will determine if a person is tense, angry, fidgety, or violent. These forces will continue to influence their self-control.

2. **Introduction:** The teacher will lead a discussion on internal and external forces, and how these forces can affect self-control.

    ▶ Make a list of situations over which you do have some control. (Discuss)
    ▶ Make a list of situations over which you have little or no control. (Discuss)
    ▶ What strategy can we use to determine the two types of situations?

3. **Identify the Skill Components:** List the following skill components on the board or on sentence strips.

    1. Identify what's causing you to lose self-control.
    2. Identify your feeling (anxiety, suicidal).
    3. Assess what happened to make you feel this way.
    4. Discuss the stressful situation.
    5. Ask for help if needed.
    6. Focus on positive outcomes.
    7. Strive for self-control (count to ten).
    8. Accept those things you cannot change.
    9. Be responsible for your own happiness.

4. **Model the Skill:** A student will come to the front of the classroom and demonstrate the behavior of a student who is exercising self-control by turning away from the teacher after being told that he got a poor grade. The class members will continue to demonstrate positive ways of managing self-control.

    The teacher will control the discussion by constantly emphasizing how the steps in the skill components can be used successfully with self-control.

5. ***Behavioral Rehearsal:***

    A. *Selection:* One student will role play a situation involving self-control.

    B. *Role Play:* One student will be prepped by the teacher to act out the following situation: The student will enter the room late, making noise. After he is in his seat, he will lay his head down on his desk and refuse to respond to the teacher or his classmates. He still continues to make a baffling noise.

    C. *Completion:* After the role play, the teacher and class will identify the inappropriate behavior they observed and reinforce the correct behavior. The teacher will emphasize that we all have "bad" days, but if we employ "self-control," a "bad" day could end up to be a "good" day.

    D. *Reinforcers:* The teacher and students will give verbal praise to any student who exhibits the appropriate behavior and correct any student who exhibits inappropriate behavior.

    E. *Discussion:* The teacher will discuss the role play with the entire class and continue to discuss the appropriate and inappropriate behaviors. He/she will ask for volunteers to respond to the following:

       – Describe a "bad" day for you and explain how you handled the situation.

       – Do you feel that if you use "self-control" in any situation it will prepare you better for adulthood?

6. ***Practice:*** Distribute copies of the following story starter, "The Switched Channel." The students will complete the story about using self-control, identifying several of the skill components of self-control in their writing.

7. ***Independent Use:*** Give students copies of the worksheet "The School Bus Incident." They are to write a short story about using self-control and describe the self-control technique used to resolve the conflict.

8. ***Continuation:*** The teacher should continue pointing out the need for this skill as related situations arise.

Name _____ Date _____

THE SWITCHED CHANNEL

Directions: Read the following story starter about a disagreement between you and your brother. Then, complete the story showing how you peacefully solved this conflict, using self-control.

You were watching your favorite TV program when you received a phone call and left the room. Your brother changed the channel and you became embroiled in a "heated" discussion when you returned to the room.....

Name _____ Date _____

THE SCHOOL BUS INCIDENT

Directions: You were involved in a serious disturbance on the school bus **but** because you have received training in the use of self-control, you were able to handle the situation with maturity.

Use the space below to write a paragraph describing the event.

SOCIAL SKILL
Avoiding Trouble with Others

Behavioral Objective: Students will learn strategies that will help them to avoid getting into trouble with others.

Directed Lesson:

1. **Establish the Need:** In order not to get hurt or hurt others, people need to have skills that help them avoid getting into trouble with others. They must learn to resolve conflicts peacefully.

2. **Introduction:** Teacher will ask the following thought-provoking questions:

   ▶ **Why do you get into trouble?**
   ▶ **Who are you usually with when you get into trouble?**
   ▶ **Where are you usually when you get into trouble?**
   ▶ **Are there times when you can get yourself out of trouble?**
   ▶ **Do you know ways to keep yourself out of trouble?**

3. **Identify the Skill Components:** Write the following skill components on the board.

   1. Evaluate the situation.
   2. Weigh the pros and cons (should you stay or leave, speak or be quiet?).
   3. Ask for help if needed.
   4. Consider alternatives.
   5. Explain your decision (if necessary).
   6. Do what is best for you.

4. **Model the Skill:** Teacher will role play the following example:

   "You and two fellow classmates are taking a test. The teacher must step out of the room for a few minutes to speak to a parent. Your classmates want you to give them the answers to part of the test, since you studied for it. You must decide what to do. You will go through the skill steps to help you make a decision. What should you do when the teacher leaves? Is it OK or not OK to give the classmates answers? (Why? or Why Not?)

5. **Behavioral Rehearsal:**

   A. *Selection:* Teacher will select five students, using events in their lives as a reference.

100

    B. *Role Play:* Each student will demonstrate the steps that they would take to avoid getting into trouble with others and the teacher.

    C. *Completion:* The class will critique the role players' demonstration. If there are corrections to be made, another student will role model the parts making the corrections.

    D. *Reinforcers:* Both the teacher and the students should praise correct behavior.

    E. *Discussion:* Students will discuss the *importance* of going through the steps to keep self-control in order to avoid trouble with others. *Note:* They will get to the point where they will begin to see that by using self-control they determine their own destinies. Teacher could then go back to the questions in the introduction and have students share some of their responses.

6. **Practice:** Distribute copies of the following word search, "Avoiding Trouble." Students are to find in the puzzle the words used in the skill components for avoiding trouble with others. When they have finished, ask them to write out the skill components on the back of the puzzle page.

7. **Independent Use:** Give students copies of the worksheet "The Day I Stayed Out of Trouble." They will write a short story describing a situation in which they would use the skill components to avoid trouble with others. This will be shared with the class at a later date.

8. **Continuation:** Teacher should continue pointing out the need for this skill as related situations arise.

Name _____ Date _____

AVOIDING TROUBLE

Directions: The following words are found in the puzzle below. They may be horizontal, vertical, or diagonal and may be spelled forwards or backwards. Find each of the words and circle them.

1. Alternatives	9. Cons	17. Play	25. Skills
2. Answer	10. Correct	18. Practice	26. Trouble
3. Avoid	11. Decision	19. Praise	27. Weigh
4. Benefits	12. Evaluate	20. Pros	28. When
5. Best	13. Explain	21. Questions	29. Where
6. Choose	14. Friends	22. Role	30. Who
7. Classmates	15. How	23. School	
8. Consider	16. Learn	24. Situation	

A	B	C	W	H	E	R	E	S	G	C	D	F	C	H	O	O	S	E	W
S	V	D	S	C	H	O	O	L	A	H	E	W	H	E	N	A	D	I	E
T	R	O	U	B	L	E	S	O	Y	Z	I	G	O	Q	O	P	N	J	I
I	E	F	I	U	V	W	R	O	X	E	Y	Z	W	C	D	S	E	K	G
F	W	O	H	D	T	E	E	H	B	V	X	H	S	R	N	E	I	L	H
E	H	G	R	S	D	C	W	P	R	A	I	S	E	Q	R	V	R	M	N
N	I	H	S	I	O	L	S	K	I	L	L	S	R	I	L	I	F	P	O
E	N	I	S	H	I	A	N	J	K	U	E	I	L	N	M	T	R	O	U
B	J	N	T	A	E	S	A	B	F	A	A	T	C	P	L	A	Y	D	G
R	O	L	E	Z	A	S	E	F	Z	T	R	U	A	P	M	N	V	P	P
C	L	A	S	S	M	A	T	E	S	E	N	A	B	Q	X	R	U	W	R
K	D	E	C	I	S	I	O	N	J	S	R	T	W	X	B	E	S	T	A
L	P	R	O	Y	B	D	D	E	C	I	S	I	O	N	L	T	T	Q	C
M	Q	U	E	S	T	I	O	N	S	K	L	O	F	V	G	L	T	U	T
P	R	O	S	X	C	G	C	O	N	B	M	N	I	E	K	A	R	Z	I
N	H	Q	U	C	O	N	S	D	N	O	C	N	J	X	O	R	P	W	C
W	O	P	V	W	C	O	R	R	E	C	T	O	N	I	A	L	P	X	E

AVOIDING TROUBLE
(Answer Key)

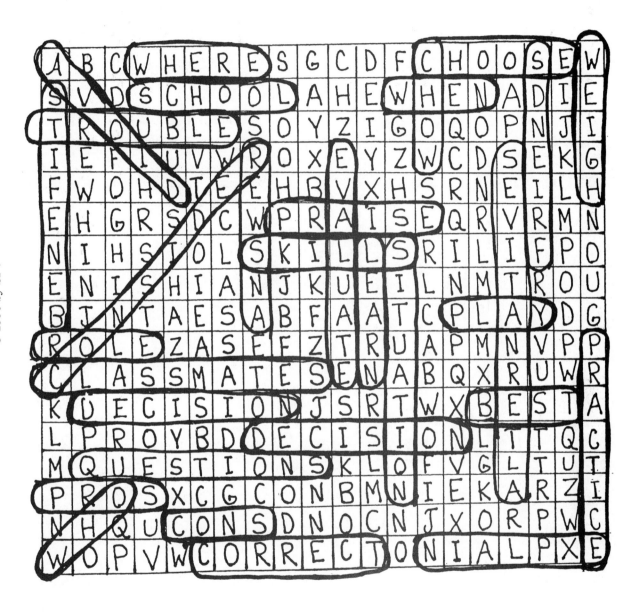

Name _____ Date _____

THE DAY I STAYED OUT OF TROUBLE

Directions: Write a short story describing a situation in which you used the skill components to avoid trouble with others.

SOCIAL SKILL
Making Wise Decisions

Behavioral Objective: Students will acquire skills that will help them make wise decisions and avoid getting into trouble with others.

Directed Lesson:

1. **Establish the Need:** People need to be able to make wise decisions in their lives that will allow them to avoid getting into trouble by themselves or with others. Students will be confronted with situations involving drugs, teen sex, gangs, stealing, and so on. They need the skills that will allow them to choose the correct course of action.

2. **Introduction:** Teacher will lead a class discussion on the following points:

   ▶ Have students take out a piece of paper and identify by name the people in their own personal support system.

   ▶ Have students write down the personal qualities and character traits of the people in their own support system.

   ▶ Have students list values that they admire in role models.

3. **Identify Skill Components:** Write the following skill components on the board:

   1. Evaluate the situation.
   2. Weigh the pros and cons of various decisions.
   3. Consider the alternatives.
   4. Explain your decision.
   5. Choose what is best for you.
   6. Follow through with your decision.

4. **Model the Skill:** The teacher models a situation in which he/she avoids trouble with others by following the skill components (e.g., she is in junior high and her boyfriend wants to have sex with her).

5. **Behavioral Rehearsal:**

   A. *Selection:* Teacher will ask for volunteers to role play.

   B. *Role Play:* Teacher will give students slips of paper with situations written on them. Students will evaluate the situation using the six skill components to help them make decisions.

Here are two suggested situations that call for wise decision-making:

- Mary is being pressured by Jake to go steady. List the "pro" and "con" of going steady. (*Pro*—always having a date, not having to risk being turned down. *Con*—not meeting new guys, always going out with the same guy.)

- Frank's group of friends smoke and they are pressuring him to try it. List the "pro" and "con" of smoking. (*Pro*—feeling of belonging, not being singled out. *Con*—expense, health, upset parents.)

C. *Completion:* The other classmates will evaluate each role player's performance. They will decide if the role player used the skill components. If he didn't, they will make corrections. Otherwise, the role play is complete.

D. *Reinforcers:* Teacher and students should verbally praise correct behavior.

E. *Discussion:* Teacher will discuss the role plays with the entire class. Review the following decision-making skills:

- Collect information.
- Organize and analyze information.
- Consider the alternatives.
- Consider the consequences.
- Make a decision.
- Carry out your plan.

6. **Practice:** Hand out copies of the worksheet "Making a Wise Decision" and ask students to fill in the blanks using the skill components.

7. **Independent Use:** Using the following worksheet, "Family Interview Sheet," students will interview their families to see if family members had ever been in situations where they had to avoid getting into trouble with others. Students shall return the completed worksheet by a certain time and discuss the interviews with the teacher and their peers.

8. **Continuation:** Teacher should continue to point out the need for this skill whenever the situation calls for it.

Name _____ Date _____

MAKING A WISE DECISION

Directions: Using the words listed below, fill in the blanks in the following sentences with the correct words. HINT: Look at the skill components listed on the board.

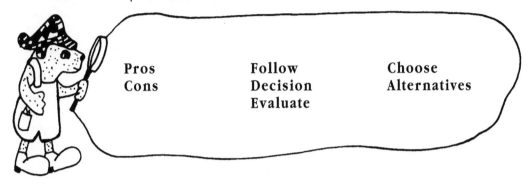

Pros	Follow	Choose
Cons	Decision	Alternatives
	Evaluate	

1. _____ the situation.

2. Weigh the _____, and _____.

3. Explain your _____.

4. Consider _____.

5. _____ what is best for you.

6. _____ through.

What are some things that YOU can do to avoid getting into trouble with others?   List them below.

Name _____ Date _____

FAMILY INTERVIEW SHEET

Directions: Interview some members of your family to find out if any family member has ever been in a situation where they had to avoid getting into trouble with others. **What strategy did they use?** Record their answers below.

1.

2.

3.

SOCIAL SKILL
Avoiding Fights

Behavioral Objective: Students will learn constructive and positive ways to avoid getting into fights with others.

Directed Lesson:

1. **Establish the Need:** Many violent crimes could be avoided if people would consider using alternatives to fighting in order to resolve problems. In reality, fighting does not solve any problem. It actually creates or builds new ones. It creates problems for the people who fight.

2. **Introduction:** Have students take out a clean sheet of paper and write the numerals 1-10 in the left margin. Then, have them write down the behavioral qualities and attitudes of friends who always avoid getting into fights. From this make a master list. Discuss.

3. **Identify Skill Components:** List the following skill components on the board or on sentence strips.

   1. Ask yourself how to avoid fighting.
   2. Ask if fighting will solve the problem.
   3. Think about what could happen to you and your partner's face, clothes, etc., if you fight.
   4. Consider alternatives to reach a resolution.
   5. Negotiate and discuss.
   6. Use self-control.
   7. Make your choice.
   8. Try your choice.
   9. Evaluate your choice.
   10. Choose another alternative.
   11. Inform a teacher or another adult.

4. **Model the Skill:** Teacher pretends to be a student who wants to have another student be his/her "best friend." A third student is also interested to have the same student as "best friend." Thus the teacher/student and another student are actively persuing the third student to be their "best friend" and start to argue with each other. Teacher/student will model alternatives to solve the problem to avoid a fight over who gets to be the "best friend."

5. ***Behavioral Rehearsal:*** Give the students opportunities to perform the behavior and be evaluated.

   A. *Selection:* Groups of three students each will be selected.

   B. *Role Play:* Each group will role play the situation modeled by the teacher and two students. They will use the skill components to help them avoid getting into a fight.

   C. *Completion:* After the role plays, the rest of the class will critique the role plays. They will identify the appropriate and inappropriate responses of the groups having done the role plays.

   D. *Reinforcers:* Teacher will give a handshake to all of the participants in the role play. Verbal praise can also be used for correct performance.

   E. *Discussion:* Teacher will lead discussion about how fighting can lead to the destruction of the home, a friendship, a neighborhood, a community, or even yourself. Teacher will also point out that movies and television shows where people are fighting should be avoided.

6. ***Practice:*** Distribute copies of the worksheet "Set Up Your Strategy" to the class. Students will fill in the blanks. Hints are at the bottom of the worksheet.

7. ***Independent Use:*** Distribute copies of the following "Rap Sheet." Groups of students will create a "rap" about keeping out of fights, using the skill components listed on the board. During the next session of social skill class, the students will bring their "raps" to the class. The class can vote on the best raps and prizes can be awarded to the winners.

8. ***Continuation:*** Teacher should continue pointing out the need for this skill as specific situations arise.

Name _____ Date _____

SET UP YOUR STRATEGY

Directions: Fill in the blanks in the following sentences using the appropriate words from the "HINTS" box below.

1. What are you _____ about?

2. Will fighting _____ the problem?

3. Consider other _____.

4. Make your _____.

5. _____ your choice.

6. _____ your choice.

7. _____ another method if necessary.

HINTS: Use these words to fill in the blanks.		
evaluate	arguing	try
choice	solve	choose
	alternatives	

Name _____ Date _____

RAP SHEET

Directions: Working with other members of your group, write a "rap" about **keeping out of fights**. Use the skill components listed on the board in your rap. The rap may be presented to the class later and a prize awarded for the best.

SOCIAL SKILL

Settling Differences without Fights

Behavioral Objective: Students will begin to see that fighting does not solve problems, but instead creates new ones.

Directed Lesson:

1. ***Establish the Need:*** Students need to learn and understand that fighting is not an acceptable way to solve differences. Students as well as grown people must use negotiation and compromise to settle their differences. Fighting in the work place, in social settings, or in educational environments can cause dismissal, problems with the law, or expulsion.

2. ***Introduction:*** Teacher will read the following story to the class:

   "Matt was really looking forward to his first summer job. His dream was to someday own his own landscaping business. This summer job, as a landscaper, would really give him the experience he would need in the future. Matt also decided he would use the money he earned to buy new school clothes and a mountain bike.

   "During the first week at work, Matt met all of his co-workers. He got along well with everyone except Ralph. Ralph liked to make fun of the fact that Matt loved his job. He would make comments to Matt and talk to the other guys about Matt. One day Matt had had enough. Matt decided to start a fight with Ralph, instead of talking about the problem. Both boys fought and got fairly well beaten up.

   "Later that day, the two boys were called into the supervisor's office. The supervisor fired both boys, since it was stated in the job agreement that fighting would not be tolerated. Matt was very upset, but he learned a valuable lesson. (What lesson did Matt learn? How will Matt react if he's ever in the situation again?)"

3. ***Identify the Skill Components:*** List the following skill components on the board or on sentence strips.

   1. Identify the reason for the fight.
   2. Learn that fighting does not solve the problem.
   3. Learn the possible consequences of a fight.
   4. Consider alternatives to reach a solution.
   5. Negotiate and discuss.
   6. Use self-control.
   7. Make a positive choice.
   8. Act on your choice.

9. Evaluate your choice.

10. Inform a teacher or another adult.

4. ***Model the Skill:*** Two students will model the following situation: Both students are best friends. They both play on the same team. One student is feeling "moody," while the other is feeling "playful." While at work, one student pours cold water down the other student's back. A fight almost starts.

5. ***Behavioral Rehearsal:***

    A. *Selection:* Select four pairs of students.

    B. *Role Play:* Each group will role play the modeled skill with these variations:

    -   First two groups will actually almost get into a fight.

    -   The next group will start with the one friend explaining that he is in a "bad mood."

    -   The last group will start with the other friend saying that he is in a "silly mood."

    C. *Completion:* After each role play, the teacher and class will reinforce the correct behaviors and identify inappropriate behaviors that they observed during the role play.

    D. *Reinforcers:* The students and teacher will praise the role players for using the appropriate behaviors.

    E. *Discussion:* Students will discuss the appropriate and inappropriate behaviors that were presented in the role plays.

6. ***Practice:*** Hand out copies of the following worksheet, "Hang Up Your Gloves," for students to complete. The worksheet asks for six ways to avoid a fight.

7. ***Independent Use:*** Distribute copies of the worksheet entitled "Cartoon Conflicts." Students will draw a cartoon how they, their brothers, sisters, and cousins could solve a conflict without fighting.

8. ***Continuation:*** Teacher should continue pointing out the need for this skill whenever a conflict situation presents itself.

Name _____ Date _____

HANG UP YOUR GLOVES

Directions: On the glove below, write six phrases that you can use to help stay out of fights.

Name _____ Date _____

CARTOON CONFLICTS

Directions: In the following boxes, draw a cartoon showing how you and your brother/sister/cousin could solve a conflict without fighting. (Use stick figures if you wish.)

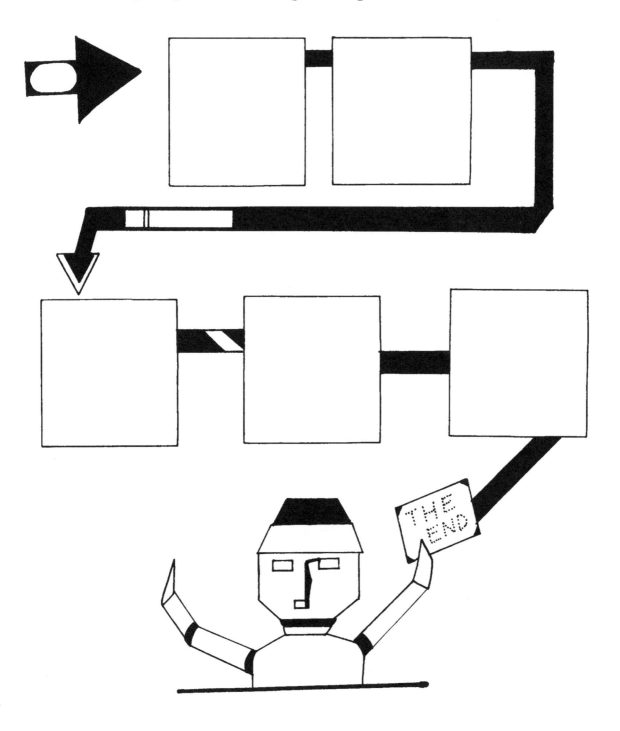

KEEPING YOUR COMPOSURE — Lesson 29

SOCIAL SKILL
Dealing with Embarrassment

Behavioral Objective: The student will learn how to handle embarrassing situations in a positive manner.

Directed Lesson:

1. *Establish the Need:* The students must realize that all of us experience embarrassment at different times. Learning how to handle embarrassment is an essential skill for social survival at home, in school, and on the job.

2. *Introduction:* Have students complete this story starter:

   "You think *that* was embarrassing, wait til I tell you what happened to me yesterday . . ."

   Ask for volunteers to read their story aloud. Let students know that they are not the only ones to deal with embarrassing situations.

3. *Identify the Skill Components:* List the following skill components on the board or on sentence strips.

   1. Decide why you are feeling embarrassed.
   2. Tell what happened that made you embarrassed.
   3. Decide what can be done to make you feel less embarrassed.
   4. If possible, correct the problem.
   5. If not correctible, comment about it.
   6. Use humor: laugh it off.
   7. Ignore the embarrassment.
   8. Assure yourself that you are all right and that the embarrassment is not lasting or important.

4. *Model the Skill:* The teacher will relate a personal story of an embarrassing situation. The students will question the teacher on how it was handled. They will discuss other possible solutions the teacher could have used. The students will also relate personal stories of embarrassment. The class will discuss how to react to each situation using the skill components.

5. *Behavioral Rehearsal:*

A. *Selection:* Choose several volunteers for role playing. (The number will depend on the time available for the exercise.)

B. *Role Play:* One at a time, give the students a situation that is embarrassing. The class will observe. Here are several role play situations:

- Your mother is upset with you for not taking out the garbage and lets you know it in front of your new boy/girl friend (3 people).

- You fall on your face while getting off the bus (1 person).

- You are the only person in class who forgot to bring a treat for the "surprise" party for your favorite teacher (1 person).

C. *Completion:* After each role play, reinforce correct behavior. Identify inappropriate behaviors. If it is necessary, repeat the role play with corrections. If there are no corrections, the role play is complete.

D. *Reinforcers:* Praise the students. Let the class applaud each role play upon conclusion.

E. *Discussion:* Upon the conclusion of each role play, the students should give verbal evaluation and relate how they would react in any similar embarrassing situation.

6. *Practice:* Distribute copies of the worksheet, "What Would *You* Do?" This worksheet asks questions about how to deal with embarrassment using the skill components given on the top of the sheet. The students will answer the seven questions for two separate embarrassing situations described on the worksheet.

7. *Independent Use:* Using the worksheet "Embarrassment Is Not Fatal!" students are to ask a family member or friend if they have ever been in an embarrassing situation, and write down what happened and what the person did about it. The student should then write (if applicable) which of the skill components the adult used in the situation.

8. *Continuation:* There are many instances in every classroom when embarrassing moments occur. The teacher can use these moments to reteach the class the skill components for handling an embarrassing situation. Or, the teacher can ask the class to relate how the embarrassed student handled the problem.

Name _____ Date _____

WHAT WOULD YOU DO?

Directions: Answer the following questions for each situation listed below:

A. What happened?

B. Should you be embarrassed?

C. Can you correct it?

D. Can you ignore it?

E. Can you "laugh it off"?

F. Can you make it seem unimportant?

G. How can you stop from being embarrassed?

1. As you walk into your English class, someone comes up behind you and places a sign on your back that reads "KICK ME - I'M STUPID."

    A. _____
    B. _____
    C. _____
    D. _____
    E. _____
    F. _____
    G. _____

2. A girl/boy comes up to you and tries to give you a big hug and kiss, and you don't like this behavior.

    A. _____
    B. _____
    C. _____
    D. _____
    E. _____
    F. _____
    G. _____

Name _____ Date _____

EMBARRASSMENT IS NOT FATAL !

1. Describe an embarrassing situation.

_____

_____

_____

_____

_____

_____

2. What would adults do in this case?

_____

_____

_____

_____

_____

3. Which skill components were used in this situation?

_____

_____

_____

SOCIAL SKILL
Managing Embarrassing Situations

Behavioral Objective: The student will learn how to manage embarrassing situations in a positive manner and still maintain a high level of dignity.

Directed Lesson:

1. ***Establish the Need:*** The students must realize that all of us experience embarrassment at different times. Learning how to handle embarrassment is an essential skill for social survival at home, in school, and on the job. The students must understand that the older you get, the more embarrassed you become. This is because you are now supposed to "know better." You have to handle it in a non-violent manner. You cannot lash out at the people laughing at you.

2. ***Introduction:***

   ‣ Have students bring in a cartoon that shows an embarrassing set up. Point out that laughter is a good way to deal with an embarrassing situation—it reduces stress.

   ‣ Make a bulletin board or chart of the cartoons and keep adding to them. This provides a "stress break."

   "One day Cedrick was approached by Courtney in the hallway at school. She told him how she felt. Cedrick listened politely. He told Courtney that he liked her but, just as a very good friend. They gave each other a big hug as a sign of their friendship. Just as they were doing this Marcella came up the stairs and saw them. They were both very embarrassed. (How could Courtney and Cedrick handle this situation?)"

3. ***Identify the Skill Components:*** Write the following skill components on the board or on sentence strips.

   1. Decide why you are feeling embarrassed.
   2. Decide what happened that made you embarrassed.
   3. Decide what you can do to make you feel less embarrassed.
   4. Immediately correct the problem, if possible.
   5. Comment on the problem and explain what happened.
   6. Use humor and "laugh it off"—so that everyone is laughing with you and not at you.
   7. Pretend that nothing is wrong.
   8. Assure yourself that you are all right and that the embarrassment is not long lasting.
   9. Confirm your own self-worth and remember that the embarrassment was not important.

4. ***Model the Skill:*** The teacher will ask the class, **"Have you ever been in a situation where you were embarrassed?"** Ask the students to relate their stories. The students will use the skill components to show how they could have handled the situation.

5. ***Behavioral Rehearsal:***

    A. *Selection:* Choose four pairs of volunteers for role playing.

    B. *Role Play:* One at a time, give the students a situation that is embarrassing. The class will observe. Here are several examples of role playing situations:

        -   Your grandmother comes in and changes the channel on the TV while you and your girlfriend are watching it.

        -   The local bully intimidates you while you are with your girlfriend.

        -   You are being escorted to the office for disrupting the class. When you arrive at the office, you find your grandmother sitting there because she wanted to surprise you.

    C. *Completion:* After each role play, reinforce the correct behavior and identify the inappropriate behaviors. If it is necessary, reenact the role play with the new corrections. If there are no corrections, the role play is complete.

    D. *Reinforcers:* Praise the students. Let the class applaud each role play upon its conclusion. The teacher should encourage all correct behaviors.

    E. *Discussion:* Upon the conclusion of each role play, have the class evaluate each role play. The students should relate how they would react in a similar embarrassing situation.

6. ***Practice:*** Give students copies of the following worksheet, "Word Puzzle," consisting of 22 words. The students have to write the words in a crossword puzzle form on the sheet. The words are all taken from the skill components.

7. ***Independent Use:*** Distribute the worksheet "What's Embarrassing?" for students to take home. They will ask family members what causes them to be embarrassed and write the answers in the circles on the sheet. The students shall also answer the question about what they learned from the survey and discuss it in class with the teacher and their peers.

8. ***Continuation:*** There are many instances in every classroom when embarrassing moments occur. The teacher can use these moments to reteach the class the skill components.

Name _____ Date _____

WORD PUZZLE

Directions: Following is a list of words that fit into the crossword puzzle below. Five words are already filled in. Fill in the rest of the words. The MISSING WORDS box can be of help.

MISSING WORDS		
all right	everyone	less
assure	explain	pretend
at	feeling	problem
comment	foolish	situation
correct	happened	unimportant
decide	humor	why
embarrassed	laugh	you
		yourself

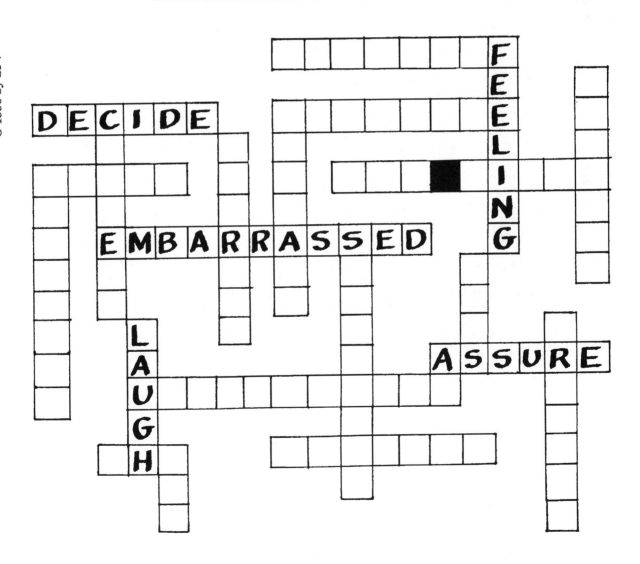

WORD PUZZLE ANSWER KEY

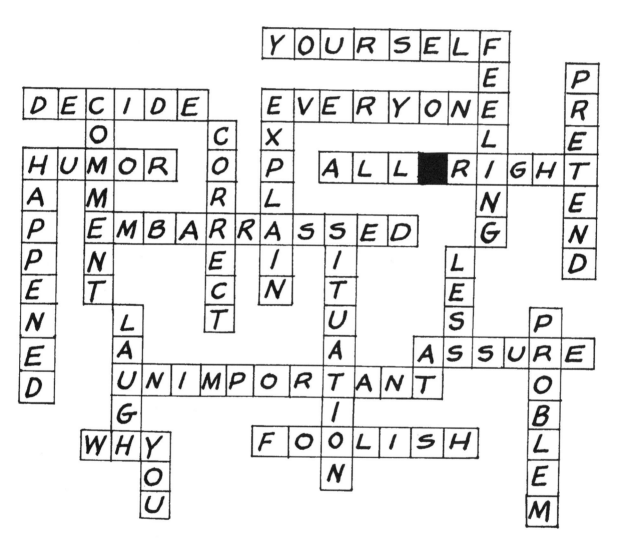

Name _____ Date _____

WHAT'S EMBARRASSING?

Directions: Ask several members of your family what makes them embarrassed. Write their answers in the (clouds) below. What did you learn from this survey that could help YOU?

SOCIAL SKILL

Coping with Being Left Out (Sex, Drugs)

Behavioral Objective: The student will identify situations where it is okay to be left out. He/she will be able to select appropriate behaviors to cope with this feeling, using the skill components.

Directed Lesson:

1. **Establish the Need:** Students need to be made aware that there are times when being "left out" of a group is the best possible situation. A sense of belonging is very important to this age group, so they must have some coping behaviors for the times when they either *can't* or *don't want to* be a part of the group.

2. **Introduction:** Teacher will select one of the following:

    A. Locate and read some current statistics on teenage pregnancy or the AIDS epidemic.

    B. Have students explore their "attitude" (manner of feeling, thinking, acting) about particular situations, such as:

    –   How do I feel when I see an adult intoxicated?

    –   How do I feel when I see a fellow student intoxicated?

    –   How would I feel if I saw my boyfriend/girlfriend "high" on drugs?

    –   How would I feel if I saw my boyfriend/girlfriend being taken away by the police?

    Students need to become aware of their own feelings to enable them to better understand their *own* behavior and that of others. In this way they will learn how to decide if a situation is such that participation with the group is justified or if it is best to be left out.

3. **Identify the Skill Components:** Write the skill components on the board or on sentence strips.

    1. Decide if you are being left out.
    2. Decide if you want to be left out.
    3. Think about the reasons why the others might have been leaving you out.
    4. Decide upon the activity in which you would really like to participate.
    5. Decide if this activity will get you or others in trouble.
    6. Decide if this activity can harm you and others in any way.

7. Decide how to deal with the problem.

    (a) To leave it as is and wait.

    (b) To tell the others how you feel.

    (c) To ask to be included.

8. Choose the best way to carry out your decision and act on it.

4. ***Model the Skill:*** Students will role play situations that cause feelings discussed in the introduction. They will find a solution for participating or not in the group activities using the eight skill components.

5. ***Behavioral Rehearsal:***

    A. *Selection:* Teacher will select several students to role play.

    B. *Role Play:* Encourage students to select alternatives to drugs and alcohol, for more lasting satisfaction.

        - Have the class members engage in physical exercise when listening to a cassette tape.

        - Have students keep a journal of their goals and dreams.

        - Have students sign up to do volunteer work for someone less fortunate.

    C. *Completion:* After each role play, reinforce correct behavior, identify inappropriate behaviors, and reenact role play with corrections. If there are no corrections, role play is complete.

    D. *Reinforcers:* Verbal praise and applause should be used for each appropriate role play situation. Students and teacher will direct statements to the participants that begin with "I like the way you . . ."

    E. *Discussion:* Discuss how well the role players used the skill components in solving the problem. Discuss how using the skill components made the participants feel more able to deal with being left out.

6. ***Practice:*** Distribute copies of the following worksheet, "Am I In or Out?" which details situations where one would feel left out. Students will complete a questionnaire which relates to the skill components to help them cope with that "left out" feeling.

7. ***Independent Use:*** Distribute copies of the worksheet entitled "Personal Log" to the class. Students are to record situations in which they felt left out. They will use the skill components to work through the problem situations of feeling "left out."

8. ***Continuation:*** Teacher will point out that once a person learns to identify situations when it is okay to be left out, then they can act appropriately, thereby reducing stress.

Name _____ Date _____

AM I IN OR OUT?

Directions: The following sentence describes a situation where one would feel left out. Think of another situation in which you would feel left out, and write it on the lines below. Then answer the five questions for the situation you have described.

<u>Everyone walks to school using the street instead of the sidewalk.</u>

Write your own situation:

_____

_____

_____

Do I want to participate?	
Will it harm me or others?	
Will this get me or others into trouble?	
Should I leave it as is and wait?	
Should I ask to be included?	

Name _____ Date _____

PERSONAL LOG

Complete these statements:

I felt left out when _____

_____

_____

_____

_____

I ask myself these questions:
_____

_____

_____

_____

_____

I have decided to:
_____

_____

_____

_____

_____

SOCIAL SKILL

Responding to Persuasion

Behavioral Objective: The student will learn to deal effectively with negative peer pressure and understand that it is emotionally rewarding to resist it. Negative peer pressure is defined as pressure exerted by peers to make you do something you know is not right to do.

Directed Lesson:

1. **Establish the Need:** It is imperative that students learn to deal with negative peer pressure. The wrong kind of pressure from peers can push someone into actions that are both deadly and criminal. The students must learn to go their own way and follow the right path. They must understand that they are in control and they have the power to resist.

2. **Introduction:** The teacher reads the following story to the class.

   "Damon had a lot of friends. He was very popular. Girls would call him up and ask for dates. He never needed to look around for something to do. He always seemed to have a buddy around willing to come up with some fun. Damon was not really poor. His grandmother and mother both had jobs, so there was enough money to keep things comfortable at home.

   "Damon had one friend who was no stranger to trouble. His name was Randy. Randy was the leader of a group of boys who were well known at the sixth precinct police station. One day Randy and two of his boys stopped over to see their pal Damon.

   "'Damon, my man, I've got a proposition for you,' said Randy.

   "'What is it?' Damon asked.

   "'I know that you are in need of some easy cash. I've got a little job that can earn all of us some spending money.'"

   Ask students what they think Randy has in mind, and explain that Damon has never really been in any serious trouble before.

   What happens next? What does Damon do?

3. **Identify the Skill Components:** List the following skill components on the board or on sentence strips.

   1. Listen to what the other person has to say.
   2. Decide what *you* think about it.
   3. Separate *your* ideas from the ideas of the other person.
   4. Compare what they have said with what *you* think.

130

5. Decide which idea is better. (Use these questions to help you.)

   A. Will it get me into trouble?

   B. Will it get others into trouble?

   C. Is it dangerous?

   D. What would my mother (grandmother) think about it?

6. Make your final decision.

4. ***Model the Skill:*** The teacher will use the story about Damon as basis for this exercise. Have the students ever been in a situation where they wanted to say "no" but were afraid of what everyone else would think about them?

5. ***Behavioral Rehearsal:***

   A. *Selection:* The student will be asked to volunteer. Each group will consist of 3 students. There may be 4 students to one group.

   B. *Role Play:* The students in each group will be given a certain situation. Two students will try to talk the other one into joining in for some "fun." Here are sample situations for role play:

      - Two students want another one to play hooky from school.

      - Two students want another one to assist them in beating up someone they don't like.

      - Two students want another one to help them cheat on an important test.

      - Two students try to convince another one to jump from one rooftop to another because "everybody does it."

      - In addition the teacher will think of any other situation that is relevant to the classroom or the school.

   C. *Completion:* After each role play, reinforce the correct behavior, identify and correct any inappropriate behaviors. Let the students repeat the role play if necessary. If the role play was correct, proceed.

   D. *Reinforcers:* Always let the students in the "audience" applaud the role play. Let the students praise all the good points. Verbally the teacher should approve *something* after each role play and give praise to correct role plays.

   E. *Discussion:* Discuss how each student succeeded in trying to resist the negative peer pressure in each role play. Comment on how well the students based their remarks in the role play on the six skill components.

6. ***Practice:*** Hand out copies of the following worksheet, "Where Is the Control?" that lists 21 words or phrases. Eleven of the phrases are items the student has some control over. Ten of the phrases are items the student had no control over. The student will separate these into two groups. The control group will go inside of "the body." The no control group will go outside.

7. ***Independent Use:*** Distribute copies of the worksheet entitled "Questionaire: What Would *You* Do?" with 11 questions in it. There will be lines on which to write the answers. The students should select someone from home (preferably an adult) to ask the questions and write down the responses. The students should return this sheet within two days, ready to tell the class what they have learned.

8. ***Continuation:*** Teacher should remind students of the satisfaction they will feel whenever they resist negative pressure from their peers and go their own way.

Name _____ Date _____

WHERE IS THE CONTROL?

Directions: Listed below are 21 words or phrases. Write the number **inside** the body outline if you have some control over it. Write the number **outside** the body if you have no control.

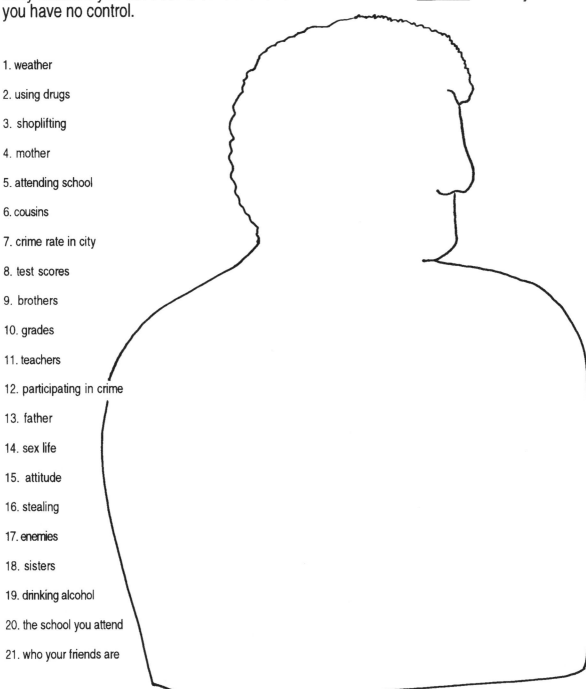

1. weather

2. using drugs

3. shoplifting

4. mother

5. attending school

6. cousins

7. crime rate in city

8. test scores

9. brothers

10. grades

11. teachers

12. participating in crime

13. father

14. sex life

15. attitude

16. stealing

17. enemies

18. sisters

19. drinking alcohol

20. the school you attend

21. who your friends are

Name _____ Date _____

QUESTIONNAIRE: WHAT WOULD **YOU** DO?

Ask someone at home these discussion questions.
Write their responses on the lines.

1. **If** someone asked you to help them break into a house, what would you say?

_____

2. Why did you say that? _____

3. Is it a good idea? _____

4. Why or why not? _____

5. Is it what you really want to do? _____

6. Will it, or could it, get you into trouble? _____

7. Will it disrupt other people? _____

8. Why do you want to bother other people? _____

_____

9. Do you want to be known as a criminal or a gangster? _____

_____

10. Who has more control or power? YOU, by saying "no" or someone who doesn't want to but agrees anyway? _____

_____

11. Why? _____

_____

_____

SOCIAL SKILL

Identifying Reasons for Failure

Behavioral Objective: The student will learn to identify reasons for failure using the skill components to develop techniques to help ensure future success in a career.

Directed Lesson:

1. **Establish the Need:** This skill is necessary to guide the student and show him/her methods to help reduce failures. It will reduce the likelihood of eventual drop-out and provide help in a first job. Failure can be viewed as a learning experience. It can mean that we need to change our outlook and our behavior.

2. **Introduction:** Read the following story to the class.

    "Bill is a student in the seventh grade. He is a very emotional young man. Bill has always received good grades in most subjects. He had been used to having only one teacher in earlier grades. In seventh grade, however, Bill had to take pre-algebra from a new teacher, Mr. Smith. Bill developed a personality conflict with him. Soon Bill began to get very poor grades. By the third marking period, Bill had fallen so far behind that he failed pre-algebra completely. When he was confronted with this by his family, this is what he said, 'I failed pre-algebra because I had a personality conflict with Mr. Smith, my teacher. I understood the work; we just did not get along! It's not my fault.'

    "Now Bill has to take pre-algebra from Mr. Smith in summer school."

3. **Identify the Skill Components:** Write the following skill components on the board or on sentence strips.

    1. Determine if you have failed in something.
    2. Think about what factors caused your failure.
    3. Think about what you could do to prevent another failure.
    4. Determine if you want to try again.
    5. Attempt again to resist failure using a new method of approach.

4. **Model the Skill:** The student will role play a situation in which a student has failed a subject and uses the skill components to solve the problem.

5. **Behavioral Rehearsal:**

    A. *Selection:* The teacher will select two students for each role play.

134

    B. *Role Play:* Students will use the role plays listed below:
- Failed to get promoted to the next grade
- Came in second in an essay contest
- Got an F in a major subject
- Failed to make the school sports team

    C. *Completion:* After each role play, reinforce correct behavior, identify inappropriate behaviors, and reenact role play with corrections. If there are no corrections, role play is complete.

    D. *Reinforcers:* Use material rewards, verbal praise, and group reinforcement to reinforce appropriate behavior.

    E. *Discussion:* Students will evaluate the role plays and discuss what it means to fail to achieve something. Using the skill components the students should tell how they should react to the situation.

6. **Practice:** Give students copies of the worksheet "A Comeback" and have them complete it in class.

7. **Independent Use:** Distribute copies of the worksheet entitled "Success Story" as a home assignment. The students are to write two paragraphs describing how a failure became a success story in someone's life. They can use newspapers, magazines, and television as sources of reference. This assignment is due at the end of the week.

8. **Continuation:** Teacher should continue pointing out the need for this skill as related situations arise.

Name _____ Date _____

A   COMEBACK

Directions: In the space provided below, write a brief paragraph describing how you came back from a failure once in your life.

When life gives you lemons,

MAKE LEMONADE

Name _____ Date _____

SUCCESS STORY

Directions: Write two paragraphs describing how a failure can be turned into a success story. You can use an example from an actual story, or newspaper, or magazine, or another source. Or, use your imagination and turn a failure into a success story.

SOCIAL SKILL
Managing Failure

Behavioral Objective: The student will learn to control his/her response to failure, identify reasons for failure, and identify ways for preventing violence and career threatening consequences. This will make the student more employable, help ensure success, and raise self-esteem.

Directed Lesson:

1. ***Establish the Need:*** This skill is necessary to guide the student and show him/her methods to help reduce future failures. It may prevent eventual dropping out, minimizing stress and depression in the realms of the school, home, and the first job. To become employable, one must stress intellectual and manual abilities. One can conquer failure by using positive thinking. It changes behavior and moods, and builds self-esteem.

2. ***Introduction:*** The teacher reads the following story to the class.

   "Jerome is a student in the eighth grade. He is often sent to the office for causing fights. Jerome has very poor reading skills. This causes him to feel a great amount of frustration. He has not had much success so far and has very low self esteem.

   "Jerome is very good with mechanics. He likes to work on cars and motorcycles. People who live near him often bring their cars to him to be repaired. Jerome has a good reputation for fixing things. He wants to become a professional mechanic. Jerome works at his uncle's garage. Nick, the head mechanic at the garage, thinks that Jerome would be a very good mechanic and he likes to have Jerome help him.

   "One day in school, Jerome told a friend he couldn't wait to become sixteen so that he could drop out of school. His friend asked him what he was going to do for a living. Jerome said that he was going to get his mechanic's license and work in his uncle's garage.

   "On Friday at the garage Nick asked Jerome to read something from the shop manual to him while he worked under a car. When Nick discovered that Jerome couldn't read, he told him that in order to become a professional mechanic, he would have to have a high school education and learn how to read.

   "Jerome became angry at Nick and threw down his wrench. Jerome went home and tried to figure out what he could do. Still angry, he refused to go to school that Monday. Jerome knew one thing: he was tired of being a failure and he wanted more than anything to become a mechanic like Nick. Now Jerome was

confronted with the fact that he could not afford to fail in school or drop out. Jerome will have to deal with his poor work record in school and with his quick temper in order to be successful."

3. ***Identify the Skill Components:*** Write the following skill components on the board or on sentence strips.

    1. Determine if you have failed in something.

    2. Determine what caused the failure.

    3. Use positive thinking skills.

    4. Develop positive methods for preventing future failures.

    5. Decide if you want to try again.

    6. Start over again, using new methods and ideas.

4. ***Model the Skill:*** The teacher will role play a student in a situation where he/she has failed several subjects and is on the verge of dropping out of school.

5. ***Behavioral Rehearsal:***

    A. *Selection:* The teacher will select two students for each role play.

    B. *Role Play:* Students will role play the situations below.
        - Failed a major exam
        - Failed to get a job
        - Failed the driving test

    C. *Completion:* After each role play, reinforce correct behavior, identify inappropriate behaviors, and reenact role play with corrections. If there are no corrections, role play is complete.

    D. *Reinforcers:* Reinforce appropriate behavior with verbal praise.

    E. *Discussion:* Evaluate the role play. Students will then discuss how it feels to fail to achieve something. Using the skill components, the students will tell how they should react to the situation. Students should not accept failure as a final situation. The students should discuss ways to convert failures into future successes in education, employment, and family life.

6. ***Practice:*** Hand out copies of the worksheet "Jerome's Response to Failure" and do it together in class.

7. ***Independent Use:*** Give students copies of the worksheet entitled "Responding to Failure" and direct them to ask a family member to share some failures that he/she has encountered. They are to record the responses and be prepared to share them with the entire class. The responses should be returned in writing within one week.

8. ***Continuation:*** Teacher should continue pointing out the need for this skill as related situations arise.

Name _____ Date _____

JEROME'S RESPONSE TO FAILURE

Directions: Listen to the story of Jerome as the teacher reads it again. Then answer the following questions related to the story.

WHAT IS THE MOST FRUSTRATING PROBLEM JEROME HAS IN SCHOOL?

_____

_____

_____

SHOULD JEROME DROP OUT OF SCHOOL?   WHY OR WHY NOT?

_____

_____

_____

WHO COULD JEROME ASK FOR HELP?

_____

_____

_____

WHAT CAN JEROME DO ABOUT HIS DISPLAY OF VIOLENCE AT THE GARAGE?

_____

_____

_____

HOW COULD JEROME BETTER RESPOND TO HIS FEELINGS OF FAILURE?

_____

_____

_____

Name _____ Date _____

RESPONDING TO FAILURE -- **1, 2, 3**

Directions: Ask a family member the following qustions and write down the responses on this worksheet.

1. Have you ever had a major failure? If so, what was it ?

_____

_____

_____

_____

_____

2. How did you deal with failure then?

_____

_____

_____

_____

_____

3. How would you deal with failure today?

_____

_____

_____

_____

_____

SOCIAL SKILL

Reacting to an Accusation

Behavioral Objective: The student will learn to control his/her emotions until it is determined whether an accusation can be substantiated, and then find an amiable solution.

Directed Lesson:

1. ***Establish the Need:*** It is important to have all of the facts before accusing someone of committing an act of false accusation. False accusations can lead to anger, violence, and strained friendships. Resolving accusations amiably is not only commendable, but it enhances the character of the person and all involved.

2. ***Introduction:*** The teacher should read the following story to the class.

    "Have you ever been accused of something that you did not commit?

    "One day in gym Frank was changing clothes and his wallet fell under the bench in the locker room. Louis was a poor and shy student who did not have a lot of friends. Louis picked up the wallet and put it in his jeans fully intending to return it. He ran out to the baseball field. When he arrived on the field, he tripped over first base and fell. All the kids laughed, Frank came over, and there on the ground lay Frank's wallet. Frank was very angry and accused Louis of stealing his wallet."

3. ***Identify the Skill Components:*** Write the following skill components on the board.

    1. Control your emotions.
    2. Consider the reason why the person has accused you.
    3. Discuss the accusation.
    4. Discuss the total situation.
    5. Answer the person's accusation.
    6. Come to a non-violent solution.
    7. Apologize if the situation warrants.
    8. Be careful of accusing someone before knowing all of the facts.

4. ***Model the Skill:*** The teacher will role play a situation in which a student has been falsely accused of stealing.

5. ***Behavioral Rehearsal:***

    A. *Selection:* Teacher will select students for each role.

    B. *Role Play:* Have the students use the following situations for the role play.
- Two students are accused of breaking a neighbor's window
- Principal confronts a student about a tape recorder that has been stolen
- A teacher accuses a student of cheating on an exam

    C. *Completion:* After each role play, reinforce correct behavior, identify inappropriate behaviors, and reenact role play with corrections. If there are no corrections, role play is complete.

    D. *Reinforcers:* Reinforce by verbally praising the positive actions of the role play.

    E. *Discussion:* Evaluate the role plays and discuss why it is important to control your emotions. Why is it important not to accuse someone without facts? What might happen to you if you accuse someone falsely?

6. ***Practice:*** Distribute copies of the worksheet "How Would *You* React?" Ask students to complete the worksheet by reading the story and writing their reactions and a solution to the problem.

7. ***Independent Use:*** Give students copies of the worksheet entitled "A False Accusation." They are to ask a family member if he/she has ever been accused of something they did not do and if so, ask for responses to the three questions on the worksheet. Students are to return the responses in writing within one week.

8. ***Continuation:*** Teacher should continue pointing out the need for controlling one's emotions as related situations arise.

Name _____ Date _____

HOW WOULD **YOU** REACT?

Directions: Read the following story and then write a paragraph about how you would react. Use some of the skill factors discussed in class to resolve the problem peaceably.

PROBLEM:

You are accused of taking a grape drink from a hot dog stand. You paid for the grape drink, but the owner was so busy he doesn't think you did. How would you try to resolve the situation?

Name _____ Date _____

A FALSE ACCUSATION

Directions: Ask members of your family if they have ever been accused of something they didn't do. If someone replies, "yes," ask him or her to respond to each of the following questions and record their answers.

1. *WHAT WAS THE ACCUSATION?*

2. *HOW DID HE/SHE REACT?*

3. *WOULD HE/SHE REACT IN A DIFFERENT WAY TODAY?*

SOCIAL SKILL

Resisting Negative Pressure (Values Ranking)

Behavioral Objective: The students will decide freely to resist giving in to peer pressure and will walk away from a negative group (peer) pressure setting.

Directed Lesson:

1. **Establish the Need:** Discuss peer pressure as it relates to antisocial behavior. Show that giving in to this type of behavior can cause much unhappiness. This can result in academic underachievement and antisocial and violent behavior.

2. **Introduction:** The teacher will do a "Values Ranking" with the class.

   Prepare the following list and distribute it to the students. They are to rank the qualities or values in order of importance to them. Number 1 would be MOST IMPORTANT and number 10 would be LEAST IMPORTANT.

- be a good friend	- have nice clothes
- be a leader	- have a nice car
- be healthy	- get a job
- have a close relationship	- have nice friends
- do what is right	- communicate well

3. **Identify the Skill Components:** Write the following skill components on the board or on sentence strips.

   1. Decide what life values are most important to you.
   2. Decide what you want to do.
   3. Evaluate what the group wants to do.
   4. Tell the reason for your decision.
   5. Stick with your decision.
   6. Develop the ability to say "no" to things you really don't want to do.

4. **Model the Skill:** The teacher will role play a student's situation in which he/she says "no" to group pressure when asked to participate in a negative peer pressure situation.

5. **Behavioral Rehearsal:** Provide opportunities for students to perform and to evaluate their behavior by peers and teacher.

   A. *Selection:* Teacher selects students for each role play.

    B. *Role Play:* Have the students use the following situations for the role play as they refer to the "Values Ranking" chart the teacher has prepared.

- Two students attempt to convince another student to assist in stealing a car for joy riding.

- Several students are trying to get you to cut school.

- Several students are attempting to persuade you to take drugs.

    C. *Completion:* After each role play, reinforce correct behavior, identify inappropriate behaviors, and reenact the role play with corrections. If there are no corrections, role play is complete.

    D. *Reinforcers:* Have class reinforce proper role play with positive comments.

    E. *Discussion:* Discuss the role playing and how well the students were able to avoid negative peer pressure that would hurt them. Review the steps needed to avoid negative peer pressure.

6. **Practice:** Ask students to complete the following worksheet, "Peer Pressure," and share their responses in class.

7. **Independent Use:** Give students copies of the worksheet entitled "When I Said 'No!'" Each student will ask a family member or friend to describe a situation in which friends pressured him or her to participate in something he/she felt uncomfortable with. The assignment will be due in one week.

8. **Continuation:** Teacher should continue pointing out the need to resist negative group (peer) pressure as related situations arise.

Name _____ Date _____

PEER PRESSURE

Directions: Write about the time your friends wanted you to participate in something and you said NO because you didn't feel comfortable. Be sure to include your feelings about self-respect when you refused to do something.

Name _____ Date _____

WHEN I SAID "NO!"

Directions: Ask a family member or a friend to tell you about a time when he/she was strong enough to resist temptation and say "NO" to peer pressure. Record his/her experience below.

SOCIAL SKILL
Making Your Own Judgments

Behavioral Objective: The students will learn not to succumb to group pressure and to use positive independent thinking skills to make judgments.

Directed Lesson:

1. ***Establish the Need:*** Discuss peer pressure in relation to antisocial behavior as expressed in gangs and gang behavior. Giving in to this type of behavior can cause low self-esteem and much unhappiness. This can result in academic underachievement, antisocial and violent behavior. Learning to say "no" to negative group pressure will demonstrate your ability to distinguish between right and wrong. This will establish your reputation as that of a positive, independent thinking person.

2. ***Introduction:*** The teacher reads the following story to the class.

   "John lives in a major city. He is a typical 14-year-old boy with average abilities. He is well liked by his peers and usually stays out of trouble. However, he has noticed recently that many of his close friends at school have been pressured to join local community gangs. Those who refused to join were harassed, beaten up, or were made to pay protection dues. He is certain he will be asked to join one of the gangs.

   "One week later, John is approached by gang members from a notorious gang. They have been accused of violent acts.

   "The gang members give John an ultimatum. Join their gang and become a full participant, or suffer the consequences."

   1. What should John do?
   2. What are the consequences?
   3. How can he get help from his supportive friends?

3. ***Identify the Skill Components:*** Write the following skill components on the board or on sentence strips.

   1. Determine what the gang wants you to do and why.
   2. Judge the request and weigh the consequences.
   3. Decide how to tell the gang what you want to do.
   4. Relate an effective reason why you cannot participate.
   5. Tell the gang why you have made your decision.

      6. Develop the ability to say "no" to things you really don't want to do.

      7. Enlist the aid of an adult you can trust.

4.   ***Model the Skill:*** The teacher will role play a student's situation where he/she says "no" to group pressure when asked to join a notorious gang.

5.   ***Behavioral Rehearsal:*** Provide opportunities for students to perform the behavior and be evaluated.

    A. *Selection:* Teacher selects students for each role play.

    B. *Role Play:* Have the students role play (variety) situations where they say "no."

       - Student groups want you to sell drugs.

       - Student groups pressure you to vandalize a neighborhood.

       - Student groups pressure you to fight.

       - Student groups pressure you to drop out of school.

    C. *Completion:* After each role play, reinforce correct behavior, identify inappropriate behaviors, and reenact role play with corrections. If there are no corrections, role play is complete.

    D. *Reinforcers:* Have the class reinforce proper role play with positive comments.

    E. *Discussion:* Discuss the role playing and how well the students were able to avoid peer pressure that would hurt them. The skill components should tell the students how to deal effectively with group pressure. The students should feel that they cannot be coerced into antisocial and violent behavior. The students should discuss ways to avoid being hurt by negative group activities.

6.   ***Practice:*** Ask students to complete the following worksheet, "Peer Pressure." Have them share their responses in class.

7.   ***Independent Use:*** Distribute copies of the worksheet entitled "The Influence of Peer Pressure." Have students ask a family member to tell how he/she feels about the influence of peer pressure in regard to increased drug use, sex, and violence and write down their response. Be ready to discuss the answers in class with the teacher and your peers.

8.   ***Continuation:*** Teacher should continue pointing out the need for this skill as related situations arise.

Name _____ Date _____

PEER PRESSURE

Directions: Write about a time when your friends wanted you to do something that was wrong. Did you do it anyway? Why or why not?

Name _____ Date _____

THE INFLUENCE OF PEER PRESSURE

Directions: Interview a family member regarding how he/she feels about the influence of peer pressure when dealing with drugs, sex, violence. Is peer pressure the major cause of these problems? You may want to discuss the pressures involved when dealing with gangs.

I ASKED.....

I LEARNED.....

MY CONCLUSION :

SOCIAL SKILL
Deciding What Caused a Problem

Behavioral Objective: Students will be helped to analyze their problems, and decide what caused them.

Directed Lesson:

1. **Establish the Need:** Students need to be aware of *what* caused their problem, so that they can focus on that cause and come to a satisfactory solution. Sometimes it is hard to get past the "blaming" and onto the actual cause. This lesson will help students learn to decipher between the difference of "blaming" others and what really caused the problem.

2. **Introduction:** Teacher will read the following story:

   "**Fred and Karl were walking along the lakeshore. Fred climbed to the top of a 15-foot retaining wall, and Karl jokingly shouted, 'Jump, Fred!' Fred jumped. He twisted his ankle and had to be carried home.**"

   Teacher will ask **"Who caused Fred's problem? Who is the one responsible?"**

3. **Identify the Skill Components:** Write the following skill components on the board or on sentence strips.

   1. Identify the problem.
   2. Identify possible causes.
   3. Eliminate factors without a cause-effect relationship.
   4. Decide the cause that is most likely.
   5. Decide who is responsible for the problem.
   6. Choose actions to counteract the problem.
   7. Evaluate your decision.
   8. Determine what can be done to avoid a repeat of the cause and the problem.

4. **Model the Skill:** Teacher role plays a student who meets his/her best friend, gives him/her a friendly greeting, and is totally ignored. He/she tries to ask what is wrong, but the friend just walks away without speaking. Use the skill components to decide what caused the problem.

5. **Behavioral Rehearsal:**

    A. *Selection:* Teacher chooses two groups of four persons each for the role plays.

    B. *Role Play:* The students in each group will be given a certain situation. Two students will go to two others for assistance.

    Examples of role play:

      - Joe has borrowed John's expensive jacket without asking permission.

      - Linda accuses Barbara of stealing her watch.

      - Chris and Beth have both failed the math test.

      - Donald and Greg were put into a detention home.

    Ask the students to think of other situations on their own. Remember to look for the *cause*. Consequences are the results of your own action.

    C. *Completion:* After each role play, reinforce correct behavior, identify inappropriate behaviors, and reenact role play with corrections. If there are no corrections, role play is complete.

    D. *Reinforcers:* Give the role players verbal and nonverbal praise (specific) for correct behavior.

    E. *Discussion:* Elicit responses from the class as to what kinds of causes there are for problems, beginning with those presented in this session: (from Introduction) impulsive behavior; (from Role Play) conflicting understandings of agreement; garbled communication through a third party ("He Says—She Says"). Ask for other causes of problems and conflicts experienced by students.

6. **Practice:** Distribute copies of the worksheet "What's the Cause?" Point out that a variety of answers may be correct, and that no answers relevant to the situation will be considered as "wrong."

7. **Independent Use:** Distribute copies of the worksheet "Problems and Solutions" to students. Again, answers to what causes the problems as well as the solutions may vary in degrees of accuracy and potential. No relevant answer can arbitrarily be assessed as completely "wrong."

8. **Continuation:** Teachers should continue pointing out the need for this skill as related situations arise.

Name _____ Date _____

WHAT'S THE CAUSE?

Directions: What could be the CAUSE of each of the following? Write your statement on the line below each situation. Discuss these with classmates.

1.   A student fell on the floor.

   ----

2.   You got a detention.

   ----

3.   Food was spilled on the cafeteria floor.

   ----

4.   A boy seems to have many scars on his face.

   ----

5.   Michael was suspended from school.

   ----

6.   Your parents won't let you go to a party.

   ----

7.   Shana was not allowed to play on the team.

   ----

8.   Sam is always getting beaten up.

   ----

9.   The substitute teacher was upset.

   ----

10.   The principal called you to the office.

Name _____ Date _____

PROBLEMS AND SOLUTIONS

Directions: Here are some situations for you to work on. Write down some possible causes and solutions. Think carefully.

1. Marvin comes to school late every day.

   POSSIBLE CAUSE:

   _____

   POSSIBLE SOLUTION:

   _____

2. Agnes is getting a bad reputation with the boys.

   POSSIBLE CAUSE:

   _____

   POSSIBLE SOLUTION:

   _____

3. You found out your friend Jose has started doing drugs.

   POSSIBLE CAUSE:

   _____

   POSSIBLE SOLUTION:

   _____

4. Vince let Thomas use his watch, but Thomas thinks Vince gave it to him to keep.

   POSSIBLE CAUSE:

   _____

   POSSIBLE SOLUTION:

   _____

SOCIAL SKILL
Analyzing and Solving a Problem

Behavioral Objective: The students will recognize problems, establish cause-effect relationships, and improve decision-making skills.

Directed Lesson:

1. **Establish the Need:** The students must realize that every problem encountered has a cause. They need to learn how to determine the causes of a problem. If you can find the cause, many times you are close to finding a solution.

2. **Introduction:** Teacher tells the following story:

   "Cindy was not a typical 14-year-old girl. Although she was very intelligent, she was extremely unattractive, introverted, and had a poor self-image. However, she did have a hidden agenda. She wanted to get pregnant by the most popular boy in school. She succeeded in her mission.

   "Bill is the most popular boy in school. He is the star of the football and basketball teams. Bill is a very confident person. However, Bill has the reputation of being a womanizer. He believes there is no girl who can resist his charms. He likes all types of girls: tall, short, fat, thin, and ugly. He met his match when he met Cindy. She became pregnant.

   "Cindy is telling everyone Bill is the father of her baby. She is acting triumphantly: She got the guy all the other girls wanted! Bill knows he must be the father: Who else would have gotten that close to Cindy? But he did not want to get that close again. Not to her!

   "Bill's girlfriend dropped him like a rock. Most of his former friends were giving him funny looks. His parents did not approve. The drugs he was taking helped him forget for a while, but now his grades have dropped and his after-school job is gone. Even other drug users look down on him."

3. **Identify the Skill Components:** Write the following skill components on the board or on sentence strips.

   1. Identify the problem and the cause.
   2. Explore your choices for a solution.
   3. Decide what are the positive consequences.
   4. Decide what are the negative consequences.
   5. Make a good choice and decision to solve the problem.

4. ***Model the Skill:*** Using selected students, the teacher models the skill focusing on a discussion of drug indulgence and teenage pregnancy.

5. ***Behavioral Rehearsal:***

    A. *Selection:* Select students for role play as time will permit.

    B. *Role Play:* Each group will role play the problem presented in the Introduction. Participants can adopt the roles of Bill, Cindy, and any others they choose (teacher, parent, boss, friend). Students not needed for role play can advise participants.

    C. *Completion:* After each role play, reinforce correct behavior, identify inappropriate behaviors, and reenact role play with corrections. If there are no corrections, role play is complete.

    D. *Reinforcers:* Reward correct behavior with verbal and nonverbal praise (specific).

    E. *Discussion:* Give students opportunities to evaluate the role play for appropriate and inappropriate behaviors. Make sure that students realize that many real-life problems are even more complex than the one presented. Point out that energies should be focused on dealing with the problem and its cause rather than fixing the blame.

6. ***Practice:*** Distribute copies of the following worksheet, "Decisions." Students are to decide what caused each of the four problems described, the effect of the problem, and who is responsible for the problem.

7. ***Independent Use:*** Give the students copies of the worksheet entitled "Solve the Problem" to take home and share with their parents.

8. ***Continuation:*** Teacher should continue pointing out the need for this skill as related situations arise.

Name _____ Date _____

DECISIONS

© 1996 by SPV

Directions: Decide what caused each of the following problems, the effect of the problem upon others, and where the responsibility lies. Place your comments in the appropriate columns below. Be prepared to discuss the information.

	What caused the situation?	Effect of this problem?	Who is responsible?
1. Ralph had his foot in the aisle and Byron tripped over Ralph's foot.			
2. Jose has been throwing rocks, and just broke a school window.			
3. Gloria and Shaleeka are to meet at 9:00 a.m. Gloria is waiting. Shaleeka just left home.			
4. A car moving down the street lost part of its bumper. Carla tripped over it and skinned her leg.			

Name _____ Date _____

SOLVE THE PROBLEM

Directions: Work toward a solution in these three situations. How do "WANTS" vs. "NEEDS" enter into the picture? Can you always get what you want if someone else is paying the bill? What other questions are there to ask?

	Is this a BIG problem?	*Cause of problem?*	*Possible solution?*
1. Sue would like to go to the beach for a vacation, but her parents want to go to the mountains.			
2. Mary wants to attend Jones College. Her parents want her to go to Williams College.			
3. Robert wants to take Kathy to a concert, but she wants to go to a movie.			

SOCIAL SKILL
Setting Goals for the Future

Behavioral Objective: Students will set long-term and short-term goals and follow the steps in the skill components to reach their goals.

Directed Lesson:

1. ***Establish the Need:*** Preparing to be successful is the best way to assure success. The first step in this preparation is establishing a goal for yourself.

2. ***Introduction:*** Have a variety of classified ads available from local newspapers and divide students into small groups. Determine where the need is (job availability). Have each group select a different occupation. Determine whether a high school or college education is required. Assuming that they get the job, how much money will they receive? (Call the company, if necessary.)

3. ***Identify the Skill Components:*** Write the following skill components on the board or on sentence strips.

    1. Decide what your long-term goal is.
    2. Get information about how to best reach your goal.
    3. Go to the library for resource information.
    4. Talk to others with a similar goal.
    5. Visit places that relate to your goal.
    6. Think about it and take steps needed to reach your goal.
    7. List some short-term goals that relate to your long-term goal.
    8. Take the first step needed to reach your goal.

4. ***Model the Skill:*** The class will set a collective goal. (Example: We will all graduate in the year 2000.) Using the skill components, list on the chalkboard the steps needed to reach the goal. Each person will then write what his/her first step would be.

5. ***Behavioral Rehearsal:***

    A. *Selection:* The teacher asks for three volunteers to serve as panelists.

    B. *Role Play:* The three participants will serve as panelists on a television show. The class will ask them questions about their career choices. The questions will take the skill components as a basis for content. (Example: Charles, did you decide in seventh grade what your career goal was?)

C. *Completion:* After panel discussion, critique responses of the panelists. Decide if questions from the audience were pertinent to the topic. Find out if the audience and panelists were left with the knowledge that being prepared is the best way to be successful.

D. *Reinforcers:* Reinforce appropriate behavior with verbal praise. Students will also experience the internal rewards that come from being self-motivated to complete day-to-day tasks.

E. *Discussion:* Discuss the students' level of performance and how well the message was communicated. Have the pupils understand that setting a goal is relevant to their present and future life.

6. ***Practice:*** Students will complete the worksheet "What Will the Future Bring?" which places them five to fifteen years in the future. They will focus on future jobs, families, houses, and cars.

7. ***Independent Use:*** Distribute copies of the worksheet entitled "My Goals Checklist." Students will discuss their goals with their family. Together they complete the checklist which asks them to compare opinions on goals and how they relate to success in class with the teacher and their peers.

8. ***Continuation:*** Teacher will point out that *now* is the time to start setting goals for the future. If they start now, it gets easier to focus on their future and easier to reach their goal.

Name _____ Date _____

WHAT WILL THE FUTURE BRING?

Directions: Answer each of the following questions about your future.

WHAT DO YOU WANT TO ACHIEVE FIVE YEARS FROM NOW?

High school diploma_____   Married? _____

Part-time job_____   Doing what? _____   Children? ____

Full-time job _____   Doing what? _____

Have your own apartment? _____   Where? _____

Own a used car? _____

Paying for a new car? _____

Acceptance to college? _____   College choice _____

A one-week vacation in _____

A longer trip to _____

WHAT DO YOU WANT TO ACHIEVE FIFTEEN YEARS FROM NOW?

College diploma _____   From_____Major_____

Master's degree _____   From_____Major_____

Full time job_____   Occupation _____

Own your own home_____   Location _____

Salary range:
    $10,000 – 20,000 _____   Marriage? _____
    $21,000 – 40,000 _____
    $50,000 – 75,000 _____   Children? _____
    $ _____

Two-week vacation each year _____

One-month trip to (choice) _____

Own a new car (no payments) _____

Help in the community _____   How? _____

Name _____ Date _____

MY GOALS CHECKLIST

Directions: Read each statement below. Place a check in the column to indicate goals that are important to you as a student or parent.

	STUDENT	PARENT
1. A comfortable house makes me happy.	_____	_____
2. I like to take vacations.	_____	_____
3. Finishing high school is important to me.	_____	_____
4. Having a good job is important to me.	_____	_____
5. Having a car is important.	_____	_____
6. Going to college is a good decision.	_____	_____
7. Liking my job is important.	_____	_____
8. Living in a clean, safe area is important to me.	_____	_____
9. I like to be well dressed.	_____	_____

SOCIAL SKILL
Setting Career Goals

Behavioral Objective: Students will set a career goal and follow the steps in the skill components to reach their goal. They will set short-term goals that directly relate to their long-term career goal.

Directed Lesson:

1. **Establish the Need:** Many adolescents fail to make the connection between what they do now and their future success. They need concrete advice on how to manage their lives so that they do not reach adulthood without future plans or hope for success.

2. **Introduction:** Teacher will ask the question:

   "Do you know anyone like this? Terence and Terena are twins who attend a school like yours. They both have spent two years in seventh grade and are now failing eighth grade. The two of them frequently cut classes, and they never do homework.

   "One day the guidance counselor was discussing career goals in the twins' social studies class. Each class member was asked to name a personal career goal. Terence shared that he planned to be a lawyer, and Terena said that she had always wanted to be an architect. What do Terence and Terena need to do to reach their goals?"

3. **Identify the Skill Components:** Write the following skill components on the board or on sentence strips.

   1. Identify differences between short- and long-term goals.
   2. Know that your long-term goal can be professional or personal.
   3. Match your interests and abilities to your future goals.
   4. Define what success or failure is for you.
   5. Make sure that your education is broad to better prepare you for overall success.
   6. Identify some short-term goals that you can begin to work on immediately.
   7. Get as much information as you can about your long-term goal.

4. **Model the Skill:** Teacher will lead the class in a discussion of what is necessary to become a lawyer using the skill components. The class will be asked to suggest some changes Terence should make either in his goal or in his present actions. Similar changes in her goal or present actions should be done by Terena who wants to become an architect.

5. ***Behavioral Rehearsal:***

   A. *Selection:* The teacher selects two volunteers to role play.

   B. *Role Play:* Two students will portray, by taking turns, a successful lawyer and a successful architect. These two professionals are visiting the school for "Career Day" and have volunteered to share their success stories. The class will ask them questions using the skill components as a basis. Their answers will reveal that they found the skill components to be of invaluable help in reaching their goal.

   C. *Completion:* After role play, reinforce correct behavior. Identify inappropriate behavior and reenact role play with corrections. If there are no corrections, role play is complete.

   D. *Reinforcers:* Correct behavior should be reinforced with verbal praise and applause from teacher and students.

   E. *Discussion:* Discuss how well the role players used the skills in their performance. Role players will discuss how they felt as they role played. Class will discuss whether they saw the connection between their present behavior and future success.

6. ***Practice:*** Distribute copies of the worksheet entitled "Career Ladder." Ask students to write down their long-term career goal at the top. Then list at least five short-term goals that relate directly to their long-term goal.

7. ***Independent Use:*** Give the students copies of the page entitled "Interests and Abilities" to take home. They are to complete this checklist with their family to see how their personal interests and goals compare with those of their family.

8. ***Continuation:*** There are many instances in the students' lives when they have the opportunity to complete a short-term goal. The teacher will point out that students should always take advantage of these opportunities.

Name _____ Date _____

CAREER LADDER

Directions: Write your LONG-TERM career goal at the TOP of the career ladder. Then, starting at the bottom of the ladder, start climbing and list at least five SHORT-TERM goals that are linked to your long-term goal.

LONG-TERM GOAL:_____

5. My last step!

4. Do a weekly check. Don't give up now!

3. Keep going. Half way there.

2. I'm on my way.

1. Here's what I need to do first.

START AT THE BOTTOM AND WORK YOUR WAY UP!

Name _____ Date _____

INTERESTS AND ABILITIES

Directions: Make a check mark if you agree with the statement.

		FAMILY	STUDENT
1.	I like working with people.	_____	_____
2.	I prefer to work indoors.	_____	_____
3.	Working with numbers really interests me.	_____	_____
4.	I like working with my hands.	_____	_____
5.	Reading is a way for me to relax.	_____	_____
6.	I plan to travel all over the world.	_____	_____
7.	I would rather be active and work outdoors.	_____	_____
8.	I like working with paper and pencil.	_____	_____
9.	I like to spend time with mechanical things.	_____	_____
10.	Working with computers is a good way to spend time.	_____	_____

GATHERING INFORMATION

SOCIAL SKILL
Using Multiple Resources

Behavioral Objective: Students will utilize more than one resource when gathering information.

Directed Lesson:

1. ***Establish the Need:*** There will be many times in your life when you will need to gather information, for example, buying CDs or clothes, writing a report, giving a speech, going grocery shopping, planning a wedding, or seeking a job. You will need to be able to use many resources of information to gain insight into all information about the possibilities you may have.

2. ***Introduction:*** Teacher will read the following story to the class.

   "Linda had $7.00 to spend and wanted to purchase a new CD. She went to the music store at the mall and saw that the CD cost $9.99. She realized that she didn't have enough money, but she still wanted the CD. Instead of using other resources that might have helped her to get the CD, she gave up and spent $3.00 on candy and gum and was left with only $4.00."

   Questions: How many stores did Linda visit? Are the prices of CDs the same at all stores? How might Linda have purchased the CD? Were there other resources that she didn't think about?

3. ***Identify the Skill Components:*** Write the following skill components on the board or on sentence strips.

   1. Determine what information you need.
   2. Consider all sources of potential information such as television, newspaper, magazines, radio, libraries, telephone books, billboards, other people, your own memory, etc.
   3. Use these resources to gather your information.
   4. Act accordingly.

4. ***Model the Skill:*** Teacher will model the skill by going through the act of buying a new television set. She would gather her information by: (1) calling a friend to see where her friend bought her TV and to see if the friend was satisfied, (2) looking through the papers for sales, (3) calling a few stores to see if they carry the brand she is looking for, (4) looking through the appropriate issues of *Consumer Reports* to see what the experts have to say, and (5) going to the store to look at the TV sets and their cost. She will finally make her decision and buy a TV set.

5. ***Behavioral Rehearsal:*** Give the students opportunities to show how to get information and how to evaluate the information.

    A. *Selection:* The teacher will select one student at a time to role play the situations.

    B. *Role Play:* Students will be given a choice of role plays. They will show how they would gather information to: (1) write a report, (2) find a job, (3) buy a new pair of tennis shoes, or (4) find out about a date and what that person likes to do.

    C. *Completion:* Classmates can give input to possible resources the role player may have missed. If everything is covered and done correctly, role play is complete.

    D. *Reinforcers:* Teacher should reinforce appropriate behavior by the role players with verbal praise, a handshake, or a positive pat on the back.

    E. *Discussion:* Evaluate role plays and discuss the following questions: Why is it important to use many resources when gathering information? Name other situations when you would need to gather information to make decisions.

6. ***Practice:*** Hand out copies of the following "Word Scramble" puzzle for students to complete. It includes many resources which students may use to gather information. Answers are given below.

7. ***Independent Use:*** Distribute copies of the worksheet "Gathering Information" to the class. Students are to take this home and ask family members to give them examples of times when they needed to gather information to make a decision. They will write down the responses and bring them in to share with the class.

8. ***Continuation:*** Teacher should continue pointing out the need for this skill as related situations arise.

KEY TO WORD SCRAMBLE

1. magazine
2. mind
3. friends
4. books
5. library
6. almanac
7. encyclopedia
8. television
9. handbills
10. radio
11. dictionary
12. newspaper
13. billboard
14. atlas
15. map
16. telephone book

JUST FOR FUN
INFORMATION

Name _____ Date _____

WORD SCRAMBLE

Directions: Unscramble the words below to identify some of the places where information can be gathered. When you finish, do the "Just For Fun" puzzle.

1. G A Z E N M I A   _ _ _ _ _Ⓞ_ _

2. D M I N   _ _Ⓞ_

3. N I R F D E S   Ⓞ_ _ _ _ _ _

4. K O B S O   _Ⓞ_ _ _

5. R I L R B A Y   _ _Ⓞ_ _ _

6. N A M L A C A   _Ⓞ_ _ _ _

7. C E P A N Y E L O I C D   _ _ _ _ _ _ _ _ _ _Ⓞ

8. S I V E L E T O N I   Ⓞ_ _ _ _ _ _ _ _

9. B A N L L S H I D   _ _ _ _ _Ⓞ_ _

10. I R D O A   _ _ _Ⓞ

11. C T I A D Y I N O R   _ _ _ _ _Ⓞ_ _

12. P W S N E P A R E   _ _ _ _ _ _ _ _

13. L L O A B R D B I   _ _ _ _ _ _ _ _

14. T A L A S   _ _ _ _ _

15. A P M   _ _ _

16. P O T E H N E L E - O K O B   _ _ _ _ _ _ _ _ _ -

   _ _ _ _

*********************************JUST FOR FUN*********************************

Use the circled letters above to complete the saying below:

IF YOU LOOK LONG AND HARD ENOUGH, YOU WILL FIND THE

_ _ _ _ _ _ _ _ _ _ _ _

Name _____ Date _____

GATHERING INFORMATION

Directions: Ask members of your family to give you examples of times when they needed to get information in order to make a wise decision. Where did they go? Where did they look? Who did they call? What did they do?

SOCIAL SKILL
Identifying Resources

Behavioral Objective: Students will use various resources when gathering information.

Directed Lesson:

1. ***Establish the Need:*** Throughout a lifetime, people will come across many situations where it is necessary for them to gather information. We live in a society where the demand for information keeps growing. People need to know where to find the vital resources that will supply them with the needed information.

2. ***Introduction:*** Teacher will present the following scenario to the class:

   If your assignment was the following, how would you find the information?

   A. You are to find out the number one song for 1959.

   B. What college did Michael Jordan attend?

   C. Where is Timbuktu?

   D. What is the latitude and longitude of Paris, France?

   Note: Teacher will entertain all responses. Have students come up with *all* of the possible places where they may locate the information.

3. ***Identify the Skill Components:*** Write the following skill components on the board or on sentence strips.

   1. Determine what information is needed.
   2. Brainstorm where information could be found.
   3. Check your resources.
   4. Use your resources.
   5. Look at additional resources.

4. ***Model the Skill:*** Teacher will show the students how to "brainstorm." She/he will pick a topic, for example, airplanes/jet travel, and go through the process that she/he would go through if she/he were gathering information about that topic. Write all possibilities for resource material on the board.

5.   ***Behavioral Rehearsal:***

   A. *Selection:* The teacher will choose volunteers.

   B. *Role Play:* The volunteers will brainstorm using the following information: A child left home at 7:30 A.M. for her intermediate school. She/he should have arrived at school at 7:45 A.M. It is 9:10 A.M., and she/he still has not arrived at school. Brainstorm all the possible things that could have happened to him/her or all the places he/she could be. Remember to use as many resources as possible while brainstorming.

   C. *Completion:* The rest of the class will fill in those resources that the role players have left out (i.e., police, tracing the girl's route to school, store vendors, hospitals, the girl's mother, etc.).

   D. *Reinforcers:* Appropriate behavior should be reinforced verbally and will lead to improved information-gathering skills.

   E. *Discussion:* Teacher will lead a discussion on why it is important to utilize *all* possible resources when gathering information.

6.   ***Practice:*** Distribute copies of the worksheet "What's the Source?" Students will list the sources they could use to find out information about each topic.

7.   ***Independent Use:*** Distribute copies of the worksheet "Presidential Resources" to the class. Students will use this worksheet to keep a "diary" on the President of the United States. They will list all the places and materials they find, hear, or read about the President in one week. The student with the most resources will be awarded a small prize. Remind the students to use *all* possible resources.

8.   ***Continuation:*** Teacher will remind students periodically to use as many resources as possible when gathering information of any kind.

Name _____ Date _____

WHAT'S THE SOURCE?

Directions: Write the source in the appropriate portion of the figurehead that tells where you can locate information about each of the ten topics.

1. Your family's roots
2. Number 1 record in 1980
3. Super Bowl winner - 1978
4. Number of syllables in "promiscuous"
5. Number 1 movie in 1995

6. Population of Chicago in 1970
7. Twenty-first president of the U.S.A.
8. Last year Yankees appeared in World Series
9. Latitude of Paris, France
10. Synonym for "ostracize"

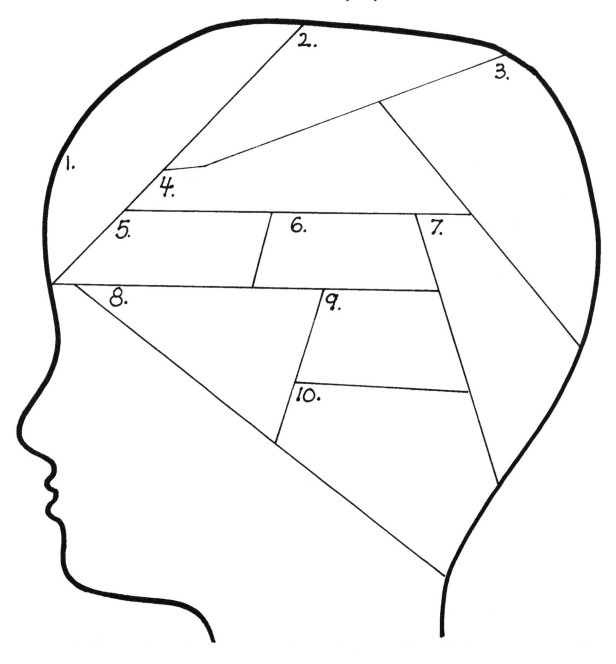

Name _____ Date _____

PRESIDENTIAL RESOURCES

Directions: During the next week, write down everything you SEE, HEAR or READ about the President of the United States. Use as many resources as possible. (The person with the greatest variety of resources will win a prize.)

IMPORTANT: Be sure to include ALL information, such as date, page numbers, time of program, etc.

SOCIAL SKILL
Prioritizing Activities

Behavioral Objective: Students will learn to prioritize their activities and act accordingly.

Directed Lesson:

1. ***Establish the Need:*** Learning to prioritize activities is a vital skill for mental, physical, emotional, and economic growth. Throughout our lives, we draw upon this skill.

2. ***Introduction:*** Teacher will define the word "prioritize." Read the following story:

    "John had three homework assignments that were due: (1) a report for his science class, (2) a project for his industrial arts class, and (3) a study sheet for a health test. John also had several chores to do for his mother. He was a good student in school and he always tried to please his mother. John was anxious to do all of his chores and assignments; however, he realized that he could not possibly do all of them in one night. If you were John, in what order would you do these tasks? Realizing that you cannot do all of them, are there any tasks you can postpone? What information do you need?

3. ***Identify the Skill Components:*** Write the following skill components on the board or on sentence strips.

    1. Write down the assignments that are due and the activities you want to do.
    2. Prioritize according to their importance.
    3. Prioritize the assignments according to how soon they need to be done.
    4. Prioritize the assignments according to the length of time it takes to do them.
    5. Begin to work on your "top priority."
    6. Accept the fact that this is a necessary skill for success at home, in school, and at a job.

4. ***Model the Skill:*** Teacher will show the class how he/she would prioritize a group of problems listed on the board. He/she will point out the skill components that helped him/her make his/her decisions.

5. ***Behavioral Rehearsal:*** The students are given an opportunity to perform the behavior and be evaluated, corrected, and reinforced.

    A. *Selection:* The teacher will choose one student to volunteer at a time.

    B. *Role Play:* Students will share situations in which they had to prioritize assignments and activities. They will explain how they actually went about prioritizing them (e.g., three events to attend to in one night, chores to do at home when company is arriving).

    C. *Completion:* Classmates will point out the skill components that the player utilized to prioritize the assignments. Classmates may then suggest other ways that the assignments could have been prioritized and done. If no corrections or modifications are necessary, the role play is complete.

    D. *Reinforcers:* Teacher and classmates should offer verbal praise. Correct behavior will also lead to improved social and personal skills.

    E. *Discussion:* Reinforce the idea that it is necessary to prioritize assignments. Have students explain why.

6. ***Practice:*** Hand out copies of the worksheet "Prioritizing Assignments and Activities" to the class. Have students complete this worksheet and discuss it during the next session on social skills.

7. ***Independent Use:*** Give students copies of the worksheet entitled "Cartoon Strip." Have newspaper comic strips available that show a character using the skill components from this lesson to solve a prioritizing problem.

8. ***Continuation:*** Teacher should continue pointing out the need for this skill as related situations arise.

Name _____ Date _____

PRIORITIZING
ASSIGNMENTS AND ACTIVITIES

Directions: *Today is Monday.* During the next week you will be dealing with the situations listed below. Prioritize these assignments and give your rationale for doing so.

_____ Three major homework assignments are due on *Friday.*

_____ Your father wants you to cut and edge the lawn.

_____ Your mother asks you to clean up your bedroom, and vacuum the house.

_____ The school skating party is Thursday.

_____ Your neighbor asks you to babysit on Wednesday and Thursday evenings.

_____ Your friend invites you to come over and listen to CDs.

PRIORITIZE ASSIGNMENTS AND ACTIVITIES	*RATIONALE*
1. _____	_____
2. _____	_____
3. _____	_____
4. _____	_____
5. _____	_____
6. _____	_____

Be prepared to discuss your decisions regarding setting priorities.

Name _____ Date _____

CARTOON STRIP

Directions: Locate a newspaper cartoon that shows a character using the skill components from this lesson.

Cut it out and paste it below.

Describe in your own words what is taking place.

_____

SOCIAL SKILL
Putting Things in Order

Behavioral Objective: The student will learn that it is essential to prioritize tasks that need to be accomplished. Prioritizing enables them to be better organized and to complete assignments in time.

Directed Lesson:

1. ***Establish the Need:*** Learning to prioritize problems or jobs is an important skill because students need to have an orderly way of accomplishing their tasks. It is a vital skill for the mental, emotional, and economic growth of most people.

2. ***Introduction:*** Teacher will read the following to the class:

    "Bryan was considered by most of his teachers to be working far below his ability. The only class he did well in was math. His mother was always telling him to try harder and work more efficiently. It seemed to Bryan that he was working hard. Usually, Bryan had homework in at least four subjects. He always did his math homework first because it was his favorite subject, and the easiest for him. His problem was that he could never decide what to do next. He didn't like English; the homework always seemed to involve writing long paragraphs. The social studies assignments required a lot of reading. Science seemed too complicated to Bryan. Most of the time, he became so frustrated that he ended up doing nothing after he did math.

    "How can Bryan get the help he needs?"

3. ***Identify the Skill Components:*** Write the following skill components on the board or on sentence strips.

    1. Decide what are your problems/tasks to accomplish.
    2. Define priorities.
    3. Write your problems/tasks down and number them.
    4. Reorder them on another list according to how soon they need to be resolved/accomplished/done.
    5. Combine the two lists and prioritize them.
    6. Begin to work on problem/task/assignment number one.
    7. Understand that you must work on the problems/tasks/assignments one at a time.

4. ***Model the Skill:*** The teacher will ask the students to name some problems they need to solve or some tasks they need to complete. The teacher will write at least six of them on the board. The teacher will explain how to prioritize problems/tasks using the skill components.

The story of Bryan from the introduction will be used as an example of how essential it is to prioritize tasks in order to fulfill requirements not only for school, but for later life.

5. *Behavioral Rehearsal:*

   A. *Selection:* The teacher will ask for volunteers to role play.

   B. *Role Play:* The students will role play the following situations. Using the skill components, they will prioritize the tasks. (Write the examples on the board.)

   Examples:

   1. A person has the following tasks to complete in a single day:
      - vacuum the floor
      - do the laundry
      - mow the lawn
      - wash the dishes
      - cook dinner
      - go grocery shopping

   2. A student is very active in after-school activities. These are the activities the student wants to participate in:
      - be in the drama club
      - play on the football team
      - get good grades
      - help teacher after school
      - get an after-school job
      - join the volleyball team

   C. *Completion:* After the role play, reinforce correct behavior, identify inappropriate behaviors, and reenact role play with corrections. If there are no corrections, role play is complete.

   D. *Reinforcers:* Praise the role players' correct behavior. Being able to prioritize will also lead to increased feelings of satisfaction because days will go more smoothly and there is apt to be less stress.

   E. *Discussion:* Discuss what happens when the people don't prioritize. Have students point out the advantages of being able to prioritize.

6. *Practice:* Give students copies of the worksheet "My Priorities Are in Order," which encourages them to prioritize some tasks.

7. *Independent Use:* Distribute copies of the worksheet entitled "Prioritizing Bills" to students. They will take this home and complete it with a family member. The worksheet asks them to prioritize the payment of bills in accordance with due time since they have only a fixed amount of money to spend immediately. The total amount of money available is less than the total needed to pay all the bills.

8. *Continuation:* Teacher will point out to the students that this skill will be of invaluable help to them during their entire life. If they use this skill, they will be better organized and more productive.

Name _____ Date _____

MY PRIORITIES ARE IN ORDER

Directions: Complete all parts of this worksheet. It will help you to set priorities.

LIST FIVE TASKS THAT YOU NEED TO DO ON ANY GIVEN DAY:

1. _____   4. _____

2. _____   5. _____

3. _____

NEXT, ASK YOURSELF THESE QUESTIONS:

1. How long does it take to complete this task?
2. How difficult is it to accomplish this task?
3. Do I need the help of others to get the task done?
4. What are the consequences of not completing this task?
5. Will my decision affect others?
6. Is there a deadline on any of the tasks?

MY PRIORITIES ARE IN ORDER.

I will work on my tasks as follows:

1. _____

2. _____

3. _____

4. _____

5. _____

Name _____ Date _____

PRIORITIZING BILLS

Directions: *Complete this worksheet with a member of your family.*

YOU HAVE THESE BILLS TO PAY THIS MONTH:

$ 85.00	Electricity
100.00	East Carolina Gas
37.50	Department Store Charge
26.50	Telephone Company
62.00	Dentist
71.00	Apex Gasoline Charge
75.00	Water and Sewage
_____	
$457.00	**TOTAL MONEY OWED**

You only have $300.00 available to pay these bills.   Ask a family member to help you figure out which bills are the most urgent and need to be paid immediately.   Do they all need to be paid in full? Work out your budget below:

AMOUNT	PAYMENT DUE BY	PAID TO
_____	_____	_____
_____	_____	_____
_____	_____	_____
_____	_____	_____
_____	_____	_____
_____	_____	_____
_____	_____	_____

Be prepared to share your thinking on your budget and method of payment.

SOCIAL SKILL
Making a Decision

Behavioral Objective: Students will review the various choices and consequences of the decision-making process, and discuss the differences between "wants" and "needs."

Directed Lesson:

1. ***Establish the Need:*** This skill is necessary for anyone to have success in interpersonal relationships, academic work, and career achievement.

2. ***Introduction:*** Teacher will read the following story to the class:

   "Joseph was a hard working young man. He was an excellent student and received high marks. Joseph also worked as a stock boy at a neighborhood grocery store, and was paid for his labor. He had worked at the store since he was 14. Joseph had always wanted to have his very own car. He had saved almost everything he had been paid at the store. Now Joseph was 16 years old and wanted to buy a car. But, Joseph had a problem. He also wanted very much to go to college. He had only one more year of high school to complete and was an honor student.

   "Joseph's parents were very proud of him. His parents told him that he would have to decide what to do with his money. They also made it clear to him that he would not receive any financial help from them."

3. ***Identify the Skill Components:*** Write the following skill components on the board or on sentence strips.

   1. Decide what the situation is that requires a decision.
   2. Decide what the alternative decisions are that you could make.
   3. Think of delayed gratification and "wants" vs. "needs."
   4. Gather accurate information about each decision you can make.
   5. Decide what the long-term and short-term effects are of each decision.
   6. Make the best decision based on the information you have gathered.

4. ***Model the Skill:*** Teacher will list choices and consequences necessary to solve the problem and to make a decision based on the information given in the story in the introduction.

5. ***Behavioral Rehearsal:***

    A. *Selection:* The teacher will select three students to role play a situation.

    B. *Role Play:* A student is offered two opportunities for Saturday employment. One job is working in a factory. The other job is in a "dance club" working as a D.J. It pays about half what the factory job pays. List the choices and consequences of each alternative, long term and short term.

    C. *Completion:* After each role play, reinforce correct behavior, identify inappropriate behavior, and reenact role play with corrections. If there are no corrections, role play is complete.

    D. *Reinforcers:* Have the class (or teacher) reinforce proper role play with positive comments.

    E. *Discussion:* Discuss the role playing and how well the students were able to avoid poor decisions by using the skill components. Review the steps necessary for making good decisions, and discuss the concept of delaying gratification as well as "wants" vs. "needs."

6. ***Practice:*** Give students copies of the worksheet "Making a Decision." Ask them to complete the worksheet and share their answers with the class.

7. ***Independent Use:*** Distribute copies of the worksheet "Decision-Making Steps" to the class. Students are to take this home and discuss with an adult how they go about making a decision, and then compare their method with the steps learned in this lesson. They will share the answers with the class one week after assignment.

8. ***Continuation:*** Teacher should continue pointing out the need for this skill as related situations arise.

Name _____ Date _____

MAKING A DECISION

Write a brief paragraph about a decision that you have had to make recently. What steps did you use to arrive at this decision?

Name _____ Date _____

DECISION-MAKING STEPS

Directions: Ask an adult at home to share with you how he/she goes about making a decision (ex., going grocery shopping, buying something new). Then, break the information down into different steps and record them below.

STEP 1 -

STEP 2 -

STEP 3 -

STEP 4 -

STEP 5 -

STEP 6 -

SHARE THIS HELPFUL INFORMATION IN CLASS.

SOCIAL SKILL
How to Apply for a Job

Behavioral Objective: Students will practice filling out job applications and/or résumés based on selected personal date, strengths, weaknesses, and references.

Directed Lesson:

1. ***Establish the Need:*** The application and/or résumé gives the employer the first impression of what an applicant might be like on the job. Neatness, handwriting, grammar, punctuation, and spelling as well as the answers to specific questions are important.

2. ***Introduction:*** Teacher says, "Are you prepared to answer the following questions?"

    1. **How do you assess your interest?**
    2. **How do you choose where to apply for a job?**
    3. **Do you qualify for the job?**
    4. **Would the job hold your attention?**
    5. **Would the job pay what you need to make for a living?**
    6. **Do you think you can get the job?**
    7. **Can you complete an application form and write a résumé that details your interests and qualifications for specific jobs?** (Distribute copies of the following Job Application and Résumé forms to the students.)

3. ***Identify the Skill Components:*** Write the following skill components on the board or on sentence strips, which you need to complete a job application.

    A. For the *application form* you need the following skill components:

        1. Obtain application form for the job.
        2. Have specific data (dates, addresses, names of former employers, etc.) available in your purse or wallet.
        3. Fill out the form completely in black ink.
        4. Check for correctness of data, neatness, handwriting, grammar, punctuation, spelling.

    B. For the *résumé* you need additional skill components as follows:

        1. When sending a résumé, always include a cover letter addressed to a specific individual, referring to special qualifications you have for the job and asking for a personal interview. This is most important.
        2. Remember: A résumé is a brief description of you; its primary purpose is to sell a prospective employer on your abilities before he/she meets you.

3. Know your interests and abilities before you write your résumé.

4. Know the accepted format of a résumé.

5. Be sure that it is neatly typed and spaced. It should have a professional appearance with *no* typographical errors.

6. Be sure that it is short, honest, and to the point.

4. ***Model the Skill:*** Teacher asks the students what types of jobs they are interested in and models the necessary steps to complete an application form and to write an effective résumé and cover letter for a particular job.

5. ***Behavioral Rehearsal:***

A. *Selection:* Teacher asks all students to brainstorm the kinds of jobs they would like (babysitting, tutoring, secretarial, etc.). Class selects one job to be used for practice in writing an application and/or résumé. Two students will work together assisting one another in filling out their forms.

B. *Role Play:* Look closely at all questions on the sample application form and/or résumé. Before you fill out the forms, read the forms slowly and ask questions if you do not know how to fill in the information. In some cases, you might want to discuss the information with the teacher before starting to write. Begin at the top with the personal information. All students, after having individually completed the forms, will share them with the class.

C. *Completion:* Each student finds a partner to work together with him/her while filling out the forms and exchanges applications. The partners use the posted *Skill Components* to critique each other's forms. If there are no modifications, role play is complete.

D. *Reinforcers:* Teacher and partners should give verbal praise for appropriate completion of a résumé with a cover letter and a job application form.

E. *Discussion:*

1. Which skill component was the easiest?

2. What questions were asked today that you could not answer? Where will you get these answers within the next few days?

3. What part of the application form and/or résumé allows you to display such personal qualities as courtesy, common sense, reliability, desire to achieve, enthusiasm, good judgment, initiative, positive attitude, etc.?

4. What questions do you still have in regard to writing the application form and/or résumé?

6. ***Practice:*** Ask students to correct the job application and/or résumé they have just completed to reflect some or all of the preceding questions.

7. ***Independent Use:*** Students will show the application and/or résumé with a cover letter to their family and friends to solicit critical comments in order to improve the forms further.

8. ***Continuation:*** Teacher will say, **"If you use the skills whenever or wherever you need them, you will benefit."** Teacher should point out the need for these skills to write an effective application and/or résumé to present a qualified image of oneself.

SAMPLE JOB APPLICATION

PERSONAL Data

DATE

SOCIAL SECURITY
NUMBER

NAME

LAST	FIRST	MIDDLE

PRESENT ADDRESS

STREET	CITY	STATE	ZIP CODE

PERMANENT ADDRESS

STREET	CITY	STATE	ZIP CODE

PHONE NO.   Date of birth

IF RELATED TO ANYONE IN OUR EMPLOY
STATE NAME AND DEPARTMENT

REFERRED
BY

LAST / FIRST / MIDDLE

EMPLOYMENT DESIRED

POSITION

DATE YOU
CAN START

SALARY
DESIRED

ARE YOU EMPLOYED NOW?

IF SO MAY WE INQUIRE
OF YOUR PRESENT EMPLOYER?

EVER APPLIED TO THIS COMPANY BEFORE?   WHERE   WHEN

*The age Discrimination in Employment Act of 1967 prohibits discrimination on the basis of age with respect to individuals who are at least 40 but less than 65 years of age.

EDUCATION	NAME AND LOCATION OF SCHOOL		DID YOU GRADUATE?	SUBJECTS STUDIED
GRAMMAR SCHOOL				
HIGH SCHOOL				
COLLEGE				
TRADE, BUSINESS OR CORRESPONDENCE SCHOOL				

SUBJECTS OF SPECIAL STUDY OR RESEARCH WORK

WHAT FOREIGN LANGUAGES DO YOU SPEAK FLUENTLY?   READ   WRITE

ACTIVITIES: CIVIC, ATHLETIC, ETC.

References: 1. Name ———— Address ———— Job Title ————

City   State   Zip Code   Telephone

2. Name ———— Address ———— Job Title ————

City   State   Zip Code   Telephone

© 1996 by SPV

* * * SAMPLE * * *

RÉSUMÉ

_____
(Name)
_____
(Address)
_____
(City, State, Zip Code)   Phone

Career Objective _____

Position _____

_____
(School)   (City, State)   (Graduation Date)

EMPLOYMENT EXPERIENCE   (most recent job first)

EMPLOYER	LOCATION	POSITION	DATES (From/To)
1.			
2.			
3.			

QUALIFICATIONS: _____

ACCOMPLISHMENTS: _____

AFFILIATIONS: _____

HOBBIES/INTERESTS: _____

VOLUNTEER WORK: _____

REFERENCES:

1. _____
   Name   Job Title

_____
   Address   (Phone)

2. _____
   Name   Job Title

_____
   Address   (Phone)

SOCIAL SKILL

How to Conduct Yourself During a Job Interview

Behavioral Objective: Students will learn to prepare thoroughly for a job interview through self-assessment and simulation techniques.

Directed Lesson:

1. **Establish the Need:** Everyone should learn to prepare for a job interview by acquiring the skills needed. Especially, one should know ahead of the interview what qualifications the job requires. Only select job interviews that interest you and where there is a potential for growth.

2. **Introduction:** The teacher explains that a self-analysis is important in making career decisions which can result in successful work experience. Before you go to an interview, decide which skills you have to offer the employer for the job you are being interviewed. The teacher might ask the student to suggest words to describe characteristics the student needs for a successful job interview. The teacher might ask for positive as well as negative attributes.

3. **Identify Skill Components:** Write the following skill components on the board or on sentence strips.

    1. Bring your résumé. Be prepared to fill out an application.
    2. Be on time (better, 10 minutes early).
    3. Dress correctly for the interview (role play).
    4. Be courteous and sit quietly.
    5. Be enthusiastic when you express what you like.
    6. Keep your hands still.
    7. Look at the interviewer.
    8. Listen carefully and attentively.
    9. Prepare, in advance, for each particular interview.
    10. Know the tasks to be performed in the job for which you are applying.
    11. Answer questions carefully, specifically, honestly, short, and to the point.
    12. Address the job duties as you see them.
    13. Explain your interest in this particular job by explaining your strong points.
    14. Explain why you especially like this job.

15. If asked, explain your future ambitions.

16. Be careful not to contradict yourself.

4. ***Model the Skill:*** The teacher might model the skill with the student as an applicant for a job selected by the student.

5. ***Behavioral Rehearsal:***

   A. *Selection:* Teacher will select the whole class to role play, with two-thirds of the class being applicants and the other third being employers.

   B. *Role Play:* Since one-third of the class will be employers and two-thirds of the class will be applicants, each employee will interview two applicants. Each employer will offer different jobs; they will advertise these jobs to the class so that two applicants can select the employer who has the job most suitable to the applicant's interests and skills. The employer will choose the two candidates best qualified for the position. Students who are rejected for their first job selection should arrange another interview with another employer.

   C. *Completion:* After role play, identify the applicants who were hired for jobs, and identify those jobs where no applicants were selected. Discuss reasons for the preference of employers.

   D. *Reinforcers:* Teacher and peers should reinforce proper behavior with verbal praise.

   E. *Discussion:* Discuss how well the role players used the skill components and how well these skill components assisted the employers and applicants in the interviews. Discuss how the skill components made the applicants more expressive and less apprehensive during the interviews. The skill components should have helped both employers and applicants because they knew which skill components were necessary for their particular positions.

6. ***Practice:*** Students should reverse their roles: employers should become applicants and applicants should become employers. Each applicant should be interviewed by two employers. Different types of jobs might be selected so that students have varied experiences.

7. ***Independent Use:*** Students should conduct job interviews at home with family and friends for additional practice and to build up self-confidence. Each student should write one home interview. The composition should specify the dress code for the particular job desired.

8. ***Continuation:*** Teacher will point out that once a person realizes the importance of being prepared, writing a résumé, with cover letter and using skill components for a job interview, they will never go to a job interview without being well prepared. It means using the skill components, bringing an effective résumé, and having knowledge and aptitude related to the job for which they are applying.

SOCIAL SKILL
How to Keep a Job

Behavioral Objective: The students will understand that it is not only important to listen to the supervisor and follow his/her directions, but also, if properly done, to suggest alternative procedures for getting work done. They will also learn that it is essential to make friends with co-workers in their own group and other groups. They should assist each other, act cooperatively and in a friendly manner, and project a neat and clean appearance.

Directed Lesson:

1. **Establish the Need:** Students have to know that to keep a job, they have to be reliable and responsible. They have to be friendly and helpful. They have the right to ask questions and get answers but should not waste time fooling around or pretending to look for solutions to complete their given task. Every task successfully completed will give recognition to the entire group.

2. **Introduction:** Accept only a job offer you can learn to handle. The teacher will ask the following thought-provoking questions:

   1. **What made you accept the job?**
   2. **Did you know you could do it or did you believe you could manage to "get by"?**
   3. **Are you adaptable to change?**
   4. **Are you flexible?**
   5. **Do you get bored with a repetitive job?**
   6. **Do you like to learn new things?**
   7. **Do you like to work alone or with a team?**
   8. **What is your job goal in the years ahead?**
   9. **Are you a good communicator?**

3. **Identify the Skill Components:** Write the following skill components on the board or on sentence strips.

   1. Learn about the business.
   2. Listen to your boss and peers.
   3. Listen and follow directions.
   4. Help others and be friendly.
   5. Check the information before you act.
   6. Think, then act and learn to reason.
   7. Keep everybody well informed.
   8. Plan, organize, and prioritize.

    9. Solve problems, eliminate risks, and eliminate assumptions.

   10. Appreciate and respect different approaches.

   11. Realize that working with people is very important in order to complete your task successfully.

   12. Make decisions only after analyzing the entire problem and considering different solutions.

4. ***Model the Skill:*** The teacher will give the task to two of the students and will help them to complete the task. The task might be how to handle an angry customer who had a ticket on an airline flight but could not get on because the flight was oversold. One of the students can be the passenger while the other is the ticket agent. The teacher will help model the job of a ticket agent by being the supervisor.

5. ***Behavioral Rehearsal:***

   A. *Selection:* Teacher will ask all students to volunteer to role play.

   B. *Role Play:* Each student will choose a task in the same or similar profession or job for which he/she was interviewed. Two or four students might work together on each task. Preferably they should select a task that they can demonstrate in front of the class. For instance, tasks in architecture, mechanics, engineering, mathematics, and other fields can be considered. Designs of parts of a product and/or equations and whatever else is needed can be displayed on the blackboard. Such illustrations can be helpful in the selection of an end product. Other tasks might be done by the students using problem-solving techniques to increase the productivity of a selected part. A discussion of how to do a better and more effective job should prove to be valuable. Possibly the class could include role playing similar to the one modeled by the teacher. Finally the students should evaluate the proposed solution, its potential for success, and its cost-effectiveness.

   C. *Completion:* After the role plays, decide if all the skill components were used. If there are no modifications or changes, the role plays are complete.

   D. *Reinforcers:* Teacher and students should acknowledge proper behavior with verbal praise.

   E. *Discussion:* Critique the role plays not only on the basis of how they used the skill components, but also whether students could have made better decisions to complete the tasks more effectively.

6. ***Practice:*** What should the student do if the boss becomes angry because the task is incorrectly done or incomplete? How will the student plan to change his/her performance and attitude so that he/she retains the job?

7. ***Independent Use:*** The teacher assigns a task for the student to do at home. It might be to repair something in the house or to fix a car, repave the driveway, clean the garage, clean the yard, etc. The students will present their home projects and achievements to the class. A family member might sign a statement that the work was done satisfactorily.

8. ***Continuation:*** Teacher will point out that people who ask for help when needed will usually get it. With help from others, the students will feel more confident and will be able to complete a task that otherwise they might not have been able to do adequately.

SOCIAL SKILL

How to Become a Supervisor

Behavioral Objective: Students will understand that in order to advance to the position of supervisor, even on a middle-management scale, he/she must have worked long enough to have gained familiarity with each operation and function. In addition to such hands-on experience, the student must have acquired administrative skills which he/she must have used for some time.

Directed Lesson:

1. **Establish the Need:** Each operation needs direction and, when others are employed, they need supervision. To be successful as a supervisor, the student must work with the team and establish a position of recognition through knowledge of all functions performed by the team and must serve as the leader with ability to make decisions. Supervisory positions call for carefully thought-out solutions that are operationally effective, cost effective, profitable, and competitive in the public market. Leadership has to be earned by treating all members of the team with courtesy and respect.

2. **Introduction:** In all jobs, it is most important to learn how to think, to reason, and—only then—to discuss the pros and cons of how to proceed with the task. The supervisor, being the leader, after listening carefully to everyone's suggestions and weighing all the consequences including cost, time, and considering the details of uncertainties, has to make the final decision. This is true for any task. It can be a most complicated, technical, numerical, or legal task, a new venture, a new marketing scheme, or even a simple job of how to successfully supervise waiters, clerks, etc.

3. **Identify the Skill Components:** Write the following skill components on the board or on sentence strips.

    1. Allocate time, money, materials, space, and staff.

    2. Have workplace "know-how."

    3. Work with your team and use other teams to assist.

    4. Teach and lead others.

    5. Serve customers in a friendly manner.

    6. Learn to negotiate.

    7. Work well with all people of different cultures and gender.

    8. Acquire information and use it to process data.

    9. Know file management.

10. Be computer literate.

11. Understand how to organize and improve social and technical systems.

12. Correct performance and design criteria.

13. Select the best equipment and tools.

14. Apply technology and logic to all tasks.

15. Be able to troubleshoot when needed.

16. Learn to effectively delegate tasks.

17. Evaluate performance fairly.

18. Recognize and praise outstanding performance.

4. ***Model the Skill:*** Teacher will be the supervisor and select three students who will be on his/her team to market new software for personal computer files. There are different channels of marketing available, and the teacher will suggest what type of software to market and what type of sales channels to use to obtain the highest market share. This also includes public relations with the media and the public.

5. ***Behavioral Rehearsal:***

   A. *Selection:* Depending on class size, the teacher will select a number of supervisors with three or four team workers each so that the entire class is participating in the role play.

   B. *Role Play:* Each supervisor will decide, with his/her team, a task to do similar to the one the teacher has modeled. Role-playing tasks can relate to different jobs, such as manufacturing, finance, insurance, social, non-profit, architecture, construction, wholesale, or retail. Also tasks can include a new venture, such as buying, organizing, and managing a store or restaurant.

   C. *Completion:* After the role plays, the supervisors will report their teamwork to the entire class. The class will decide if all skill components were used by each team and suggest modifications and changes, if needed. After all modifications are made, role play is complete.

   D. *Reinforcers:* Appropriate teamwork should be acknowledged by verbal praise and positive comments from the teacher and peers.

   E. *Discussion:* The discussion groups might take issue with the tasks chosen by the supervisors and the attitude of the team workers with each other and the supervisor. The entire class will not only critique the teamwork but also the job choice they made. In some cases, the class might arrive at different alternative solutions.

6. ***Practice:*** Let us assume that in one case, the team did not follow the decision made by the supervisor, even after negotiations. Maybe one person in the team was responsible for not following the supervisor's suggestions. What action should the supervisor and the team members take if:

   The task was completed successfully?

   The task could not be completed?

   The task was completed but time and cost were both too high?

7. ***Independent Use:*** Teacher asks the entire class to critique the different tasks of the various teams and grade the supervisors, the teams, and the individual team workers for their contributions. Each student should also grade the value of each task and note which tasks have been handled by using the skill components.

8. ***Continuation:*** It is only necessary to see a task through to completion, but the students must keep in mind that the product must be marketable, profitable, and cost effective.

SOCIAL SKILL
Code of Job Ethics—Part of Job Skills

Behavioral Objective: Students will learn that teamwork, working together, and making decisions are the most important job skills. The Code of Ethics for working successfully together requires working in harmony with both men and women from diverse cultural and economic backgrounds. Young people have to acquire the skills for judging and dealing fairly with others and make them as much a part of their education as the learning of reading and writing skills.

Directed Lesson:

1. **Establish the Need:** Students must know that as far as the job is concerned, they should treat everyone as equals. Legal and ethical means should be used to achieve legal and ethical ends. In all jobs, it is most important to treat everyone as you would want to be treated; i.e., politely, courteously, and in a friendly manner. Try to learn from others and try to understand that having different opinions can be advantageous.

2. **Introduction:** People should be motivated to perform well the jobs they are given to do. Some people may not do what is wanted since they are individuals and thus have different feelings, and you must make yourself understood by them. The dignity of each individual should be respected. By explaining patiently to an individual why a job should be done at a certain time, in sequence and in the manner you request, he/she might come around to understand and cooperate.

3. **Identify Skill Components:** Write the following skill components on the board or on sentence strips.

    1. Set an example of what you expect from others.
    2. Treat all equally according to their qualifications.
    3. Emphasize the future rather than the past.
    4. Deal with causes and not with symptoms.
    5. Learn from mistakes.
    6. Do not pass the buck.
    7. Consider difficult and easy results.
    8. Assure that everyone involved benefits.
    9. Maximize an employee's potential.
    10. Praise achievements.
    11. Promote good human relations.
    12. Create trust and confidence in a diverse group.

13. Do not show preference.

14. Promote people when they deserve it.

15. Show concern for an employee's difficult behavior.

16. Assist all employees to adjust.

17. Take time to counsel all employees.

4. ***Model the Skill:*** The teacher will model the skill by showing the same respect to all persons in his/her group, in the same manner. To model the role play, the teacher will ask one person, either a man or a woman, from each culture in his/her group to join in a discussion about the equal, as well as the unique, characteristics of the human species. The teacher will attempt to make everyone realize that they will be judged by performance only. Persons with equal jobs will receive equal space and equal treatment. No favoritism will be tolerated.

The four persons are sales clerks in a department store. The African-American complains that the Asian-American woman has the easier job. The other two also have complaints. The teacher will solve the problem by suggesting that each of them do the job of the other for one week. After this, a discussion will show that the teacher, being the supervisor, did not show any preference. To prove this, the teacher will permit the four persons to select their preferred job. If more than one person likes a job better than another job, the supervisor will schedule the employees to do the job by sequential, monthly schedules. This, of course, can only be done if all four persons have the same skill and effectiveness in dealing with customers.

5. ***Behavioral Rehearsal:***

A. *Selection:* Teacher will ask to role play three groups of five students where the three groups consist of persons with different cultural and environmental backgrounds.

B. *Role Play:* One of the five in each group is the supervisor while the other four are employees. The three supervisors will be selected also from different cultural and environmental backgrounds. The role play will be similar to the one modeled by the teacher. If the four employees feel that they are not being treated equally, the supervisor has to either explain the difference in their qualifications or invent a scheme to give all the same opportunities. The jobs can be workers, teachers, engineers, nurse's aides, etc. The use of the skill components might be helpful.

C. *Completion:* The class will critique the role plays and specially consider the ethical behavior of the supervisors. If the class does not agree with the actions of the supervisors, they have to recommend what should have been done instead. If the skill components were used properly and no further modifications are suggested, the role plays are complete.

D. *Reinforcers:* Proper ethical behavior should be reinforced by teacher and peers.

E. *Discussion:* Teacher will discuss the role play by pointing out how difficult it is to make all persons believe that they are being treated fairly. He/she also will point out that not everyone can be treated equally since persons are differently qualified. They are also different in aptitude and behavior. Frequently the interest in a job and work is not the same, thus performance differs. Motivation might help.

6. ***Practice:*** Describe two workers out of the role play who could not be treated equally because of differences in know-how, in behavior, speech, qualifications, dress code, aptitude, interest and reliability, etc.

7. ***Independent Use:*** Students will look at their friends to find out if they are treated equally for equal performance. If they are not treated equally, they will determine what the actual reasons were for unequal treatment.

8. ***Continuation:*** The teacher will point out that our judgment of what is fair treatment will be more reliable when we apply the skill components in all job and work situations.

Part I of the following "Social Skills Task Review" presents 40 social skills-related questions in worksheet form. You may reproduce the worksheet pages as many times as needed and use them to introduce the study of social skills as well as to assess the effectiveness of a lesson after a social skills lesson and activity has been completed. The Task Review questions may also serve as topics for discussion. Appropriate questions can be presented to the students before studying a particular skill, such as dealing with feelings, and, later following the lesson, to see how students' thinking may have changed.

Name _____ Date _____

TASK REVIEW
Part I

Directions: Answer each question in a complete sentence.

1. What are social skills?_____
   _____
   _____

2. Why is listening important?_____
   _____

3. Why is it important to set goals?_____
   _____

4. Why is it important to complete assignments?_____
   _____
   _____

5. Why is it important to pay attention and not let other things distract you?_____
   _____

6. Why is it important to follow instructions and directions?_____
   _____
   _____

7. Why is problem solving so important?_____
   _____
   _____

8. Whose advice do you trust?_____
   _____

9. Is conflict a part of life?_____
   _____

TASK REVIEW
(Continued)

10. Are there two sides to every conflict?_____

    _____

11. Do you realize why inappropriate behavior can cause conflict?_____

    _____

12. How can behavior and attitude be changed?_____

    _____

13. How do you settle conflicts without violence?_____

    _____

14. What do you achieve by fighting?_____

    _____

15. How do you avoid getting into a fight?_____

    _____

16. Does it take a lot of practice and skill to learn to handle conflicts constructively?

    _____

    _____

17. Why is it important to accept consequences in a graceful manner?_____

    _____

18. Why is it necessary to react to failure?_____

    _____

19. Why is self-image important? Does it give you self-esteem?_____

    _____

20. Why should you understand your own feelings?_____

    _____

TASK REVIEW
(Continued)

21. Why should you show understanding of another's feelings?_____
_____

22. Why does it help to talk over feelings with other people you trust?_____
_____

23. What does self-respect mean to you?_____
_____

24. Why is it important to get or make a deserved compliment?_____
_____

25. Why is it important to ask permission politely if you want to borrow anything?
_____
_____

26. Why does it help you to work *with* others?_____
_____

27. List all actions you consider good for you and good for others._____
_____
_____

28. List all actions you should avoid because they might harm others._____
_____
_____

29. Why would you like to do something for someone else?_____
_____
_____

30. How do you treat a person you dislike?_____
_____

TASK REVIEW
(Continued)

31. Why is self-control important?_____

_____

_____

32. Why is dealing with anger important?_____

_____

33. Why is dealing with another's anger important?_____

_____

_____

34. What is your response when somebody insults or teases you?_____

_____

35. List things that make you angry._____

_____

36. How do you respond when somebody gets angry with you?_____

_____

_____

37. Can you find constructive means to release anger?_____

_____

38. Why is dealing with group pressure important? How do you handle it?

_____

_____

39. Are group pressure, self-esteem, and self-control related?_____

_____

_____

40. How do you make decisions?_____

_____

SOCIAL SKILLS TASK REVIEW Part II

Directions: Display the following social skills-related words on a colorful chart with a catchy title such as that used in the example on the following page.

Discuss one word with the students each day, then review the words using a procedure such as one of these:

▶ Have a student use a pointer, point to a word, and explain what it means.

▶ Have a student point to a word and ask one of his/her classmates to explain that word's meaning.

▶ Have a student give the meaning of a word and ask a classmate to correctly identify the correct word.

Words	*Sample Explanation*
Social Skills	what we need to get along with others
Conflict	a disagreement in ideas or interests
Attitude	how we think and act about someone or something
Compromise	an agreement in which each side gives up some demands or desires
Listening	to pay attention to what others are saying
Self-Image	how we think and feel about ourself and our abilities
Values	what we and others think are important and desirable to have
Peer Pressure	what our friends and peers want us to do
Negative Peer Pressure	what our peers want us to do but what is not right to do
Violence	fighting, shooting, hitting, and more
Non-Violence	discussing, talking quietly, and more

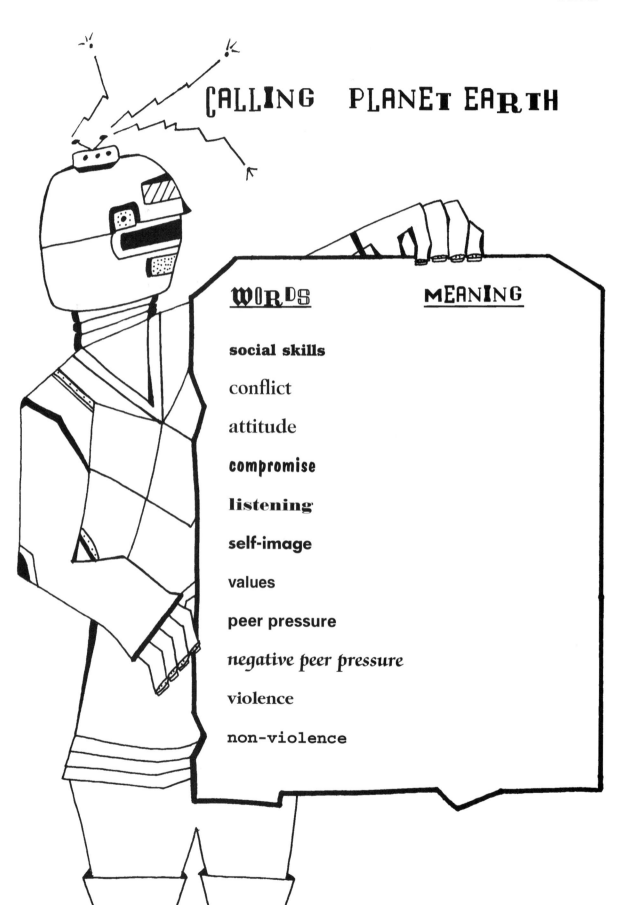

CALLING PLANET EARTH

WORDS

MEANING

social skills

conflict

attitude

compromise

listening

self-image

values

peer pressure

negative peer pressure

violence

non-violence

APPENDIX

Book References Related to Specific Lessons

THINKING BEFORE ACTING

Avi. *Nothing But the Truth: A Documentary Novel.* Orchard Books, 1991.

Fox, Paula. *One-Eyed Cat.* Bradbury, 1984.

Paterson, Katherine. *Bridge to Teribithia.* Crowell, 1977.

Raskin, Ellen. *The Westing Game.* Avon Books, 1978.

LISTENING TO OTHERS

Avi. *Blue Heron.* Bradbury Press, 1992.

George, Jean Craighead. *Julie.* Harper Collins, 1994.

Hoe, Diane. *Slow Dance.* Scholastic, 1989.

FOLLOWING DIRECTIONS

Hentoff, Nat. *The Day They Came to Arrest the Book.* Dell, 1982.

Spinelli, Jerry. *There's A Girl in My Hammerlock.* Simon & Schuster, 1991.

IMPROVING SELF-IMAGE

Beckwith, Lillian. *The Spuddy.* Dell, 1974.

Paulsen, Gary. *Hatchet.* Bradbury, 1987.

_____. *The River.* Dell Publishing, 1991.

Voight, Cynthia. *The Runner.* Atheneum, 1985.

ACCEPTING CONSEQUENCES

Lowry, Lois. *Your Move, J. P.* Houghton Mifflin, 1990.

Rhue, Morton. *The Wave.* Dell, 1981.

Sonnenmark, Laura A. *Something's Rotten in the State of Denmark.* Scholastic, 1990.

PROBLEM SOLVING

Meyer, Carolyn. *Denny's Tapes.* Margaret K. McElderry, 1987.

Petersen, P. J. *Would You Settle for Improbable?* Dell, 1981.

Ure, Jean. *What If They Saw Me Now?* Dell, 1985.

SELF-CONTROL

Greenberg, Jan. *The Pig-Out Blues.* Dell, 1982.

Holland, Isabelle. *Heads You Win, Tails I Lose.* Laurel Leaf, 1973.

Moore, Emily. *Whose Side Are You On?* Farrar, Straus & Giroux, 1988.

FEELINGS

Grant, Cynthia D. *Phoenix Rising, or How to Survive Your Life.* Atheneum, 1989.

Mahy, Margaret. *The Catalogue of the Universe.* Atheneum, 1985.

Myers, Walter Dean. *Fast Sam, Cool Clyde, and Stuff.* Puffin, 1988.

_____. *Won't Know Till I Get There.* Puffin, 1982.

Naylor, Phyllis Reynolds. *Shiloh.* Dell, 1991.

Peck, Richard. *Close Enough to Touch.* Delacorte, 1981.

Rosenberg, Ellen. *Growing Up Feeling Good, A Growing Up Handbook Especially for Kids.* Puffin, 1987.

RESPECT FOR OTHERS

Byars, Betsy. *Summer of the Swans.* Viking Press, 1970.

Landis, J. D. *Looks Aren't Everything.* Bantam, 1990.

Polacco, Patricia. *Pink and Say.* Philomel, 1994.

ACCEPTING DIFFERENCES

Ryan, Mary E. *My Sister Is Driving Me Crazy.* Simon & Schuster, 1991.

Spinelli, Jerry. *Maniac Magee.* Little Brown, 1990.

Weyn, Suzanne. *The Makeover Summer.* Avon, 1988.

PEER PRESSURE

Alcock, Vivien. *The Trial of Anna Cotman.* Delacorte, 1990.

Bach, Alice. *The Meat in the Sandwich.* Dell, 1975.

Cormier, Robert. *We All Fall Down.* Delacorte, 1991.

Larimer, Tamela. *Buck.* Avon, 1986.

Morris, Winifred. *Dancer in the Mirror.* Atheneum, 1987.